ExtraVagance

Extravagance

THE WORLD OF WHIMSICAL INTERIORS

ROLAND BEAUFRE   CLAUDE BERTHOD

Flammarion

To the man who shares my home, my life, and my loves
CLAUDE BERTHOD

To my nieces, Eugénie and Blanche
ROLAND BEAUFRE

Contents

Fiat Luxury

*W*ell, of course, it *can* be a family thing. Like running to fat or a bald patch, say. But one can never be sure: extravagance is not a genetic defect. Nor a gift from on high. No-one is born extravagant: you have to work at it. It can be a reaction, a suit of armor you wear to protect yourself from tedium or boredom. A provocation, too, in defiance of one's peers. Or even a profession, if you go in for selling things or ideas, because in avant-garde and marginal markets, it pays to exploit rarity a bit—it hikes up the price.

Extravagance was long believed a British specialty, like candlewick bedspreads, bowler hats, and humor. This is because, as Edith Sitwell, an expert if ever there was one on this topic, opined in 1933, the English are so thoroughly convinced of their infallibility that what other people think of them is simply irrelevant. Perhaps extravagance—following gin and tweed—has been the subject of an export drive; or perhaps in some corners of Europe, people have simply become audacious enough to show off what a few years ago might have been hidden away. Today, trying to turn the heads of passers-by with sartorial outlandishness is a thankless task, as is attempting to outrage one's readers with the narrative of some choice perversion. The only space left is that behind closed doors: nowadays, it is only in the privacy of one's own home that it is possible to give full vent to one's lunacy. And in this area, there *are* barriers to be broken down and traditions that need a new lick of paint.

Specialist antique shops possess an ample supply of furniture, paintings, fittings, indeed of everything you might need to resurrect a vanished world or realize your most off-the-wall daydreams. Most people, however, and this includes most interior designers, are glad merely to raid the inexhaustible storeroom and release historical cover versions as uninspiring as they are unscientific. This is the antipode of extravagance which, as the French humanist Montaigne noted in 1580, consists in "escaping from the norm." Ludwig II of Bavaria, for one, lost his *Schlösser*, fortune, crown, and mind playing at that little game. The Facteur Cheval spent thirty years of his life picking up pebbles off the street and building them into an uninhabitable Palace. Both succeeded in what was Dalí's ambition too: "To become unforgettable." Our own

Dennis Severs fell in love with this abandoned Georgian townhouse in London. He restored and decorated it with paintings in the style of the period. RIGHT: the show begins in the staircase. FOLLOWING PAGE: a sumptuous display of blue Chinese porcelain around the fireplace.

"Extravagants" do not necessarily aim so high. They simply feel the need, here and now, to live differently. And, since they are themselves so individual, their houses that resemble them do not at all resemble each other. Extravagance, then, is not a style, it's a mindset.

Extravagance is often absorbed into the baroque, that culture of excess, excrescence, overflow, and theatricality. What purists denounce as being ostentation, psychologists on the contrary diagnose as timidity, as a way of shielding the personality behind objects. Those who feel the heartfelt need for a protective shell so as to be able to be themselves, and who do not shrink before stacks of bibelots, piles of fabric, and heaps of cushions, call "deserted" apartments from which "ornament" (as Alfred Loos termed the *bête noire* of his utilitarian crusade) has been banished unlivable—and thus, extravagant. For other minds, the acme of boredom is represented by petrified mansions, those funerary monuments erected to the glory of Louis XV, Empire or Art-Deco styles that leave no room for the imagination. Fancy, liberty, diversity—these are the things that our chosen Extravagants stand for. We have not found their like among the super-rich: there are no more Chanels or Schiaparellis to parade unconventional interiors with inimitable panache. Their successors, even those of the most fabulous wealth, do little else than watch the share price rise, buying, selling, merging, sponsoring, downsizing, and restructuring, leaving a professional marvelously acquainted with the arts of patina and distressing to resurrect past salons in which they have no time to receive, to decorate bedrooms in which they have no time to sleep, to equip kitchens in which they will never lift so much as a spoon.

So, having excluded these hardly magnetic magnates, as well as inveterate collectors cowering behind their treasures and stars so busy moving and shaking they scarcely have a home to call their own, if we set aside for a moment all the flats in which tenants, impoverished as to both money and imagination, fight a losing battle, and nice enough two-up two-downs whose gimmicks and "space-saving ideas" take up too much space in lifestyle magazines, what are we left with exactly? Only the genuine creative spirit of designers, architects, painters, sculptors, and stylists. Even then, this doesn't include the ones who have sacrificed their lives to their international careers and camp out in hotels and airports with only a briefcase for company. What's more they have to be prepared to open their doors to a photographer—some of them think of a picture as tantamount to a violation. And to cohabit with other creatives in the pages of a single book—everyone thinks they are unique.

The ones we have met with, listened to, and whose stories we tell here have had the grace to accept the conditions. Our aesthetic investigations have thus become a kind of walk, half on the wild side and half down memory lane. And we've brought back over a hundred snapshots that document taste and offer an invitation to follow one's own ideas and construct an interior without fear of showing one's vulnerability, of making mistakes, of self-contradiction.

Like Pierre Loti, one could juxtapose in the exact same space unbridled exoticism and reined-in asceticism. One could become enamoured of one style only to throw it over and cast what one has adored into the flames. It's not that rare a phenomenon; Pinto, it is said, chucked out his nineteenth-century luxuries to make space for a handful of marvels of the 1930s (that would have been some bonfire).

Andy Warhol is another animal entirely, the only artist able to challenge the eccentric supremacy of Salvador Dalí himself. Having summarily decreed that a sure sign of being rich was to have enormous amounts of empty space, Warhol spent the last years of his life in a twenty-seven-room city residence stuffed with priceless knick-knacks and designer jewelry. The sale that took place at Sotheby's, New York, in May 1988, exceeded its wildest estimates. Perhaps it might be said that—with a garish puppet fetching 77,000 dollars and a drawing of an electric lightbulb signed Jasper Johns being nabbed for more than 242,000 dollars—world records for extravagance are set at auctions. But perhaps there are other words that better describe the incestuous relationship between art and money.

Claude Berthod

Loti's Exotic Labyrinth

When, at the close of a Dior show, John Galliano is about to come on stage to salute his public, the audience holds its breath. In what guise will he appear—As a boxer? Marquis? Tango dancer? Roman emperor? The spectators—international store buyers, fashion journalists—may well be the most blasé imaginable, but some are struck dumb at the sight. Is he brilliant? Ridiculous? Outrageous? What is one to make of it all? What can one say? Or write?

One can only imagine the reaction that greeted one of Galliano's forerunners one hundred years ago, a man in the habit of receiving visitors in costume and make-up, each get-up more astonishing than the one before. His name: Pierre Loti. Yet, before he was able to enjoy life in a house that he'd designed like a theater, with its own props department and costumes room, he first had to find a way of earning his keep. He had to choose a stage upon which to play out his life. And a role to fit him.

Third child of a middle-class family, Julien Viaud was born at Rochefort in 1850, and grew up in a house belonging to his maternal grandfather. If the little town's austere streets—laid out straight as arrows by Colbert—hardly waited for sundown before emptying completely, it was only because the quayside of the River Charente, with its barracks, arsenal, and boisterous taverns already teemed with people. This was everyone's favorite haunt, especially for young men on the hunt for adventure: there, merchants, travelers, and explorers would cross paths every day, exchanging stories perfectly designed to fire any fifteen-year-old imagination.

Like many of his pals, Julien set his sights on going to sea. Officer class, of course, so Father and Mother wouldn't be too put out, and also so as to live up to his elder brother, Gustave, a naval surgeon.

What with casting off and weighing anchor, building up and knocking down,

The most spectacular rooms in the exotic and eclectic maze that is Pierre Loti's house
are the Turkish Salon, the mosque, and Arab Chamber, packed to the rafters with mosaics,
carpets, cushions, and stools.

*The various spaces
of the mosque, the most splendid
room in the house,
are divided by colonnades.*

FOLLOWING PAGES: a view of the Turkish Salon in which Loti would receive guests in an atmosphere lit by candles and oil lamps; a coffee service and a Persian peacock stand on chased copper side tables of Syrian origin.

after passing out of French Naval College in 1867, Julien Viaud's life could hardly be described as plain sailing. Indeed, it was the sea, with its winds and waves, storms and dog days, that gave his existence any direction and rhythm it had. Then there was the writing of course. The house on rue Saint-Pierre served as home port, with its Red Salon lined with family portraits, and a miniature museum containing a child's booty of shells and trinkets.

His first earnings soon repurchased the family house for his mother who had fallen into debt. At home once more, Loti transformed the notes he'd scribbled in various cabins during his expeditions into bestsellers. This is a common enough process among writers. More unusual is that the revamped, refurbished, and enlarged house—a second, then a third building were gradually added—was to become the true masterpiece of an author who today is read by the few, but visited by the many. It was this three-dimensional autobiography, chock-a-block with souvenirs and finds, passions and obsessions, that Julien Viaud bequeathed to his son, Samuel, in 1923.

In 1871, the year he became the house's owner, Julien also brought back from his ports of call on Easter Island and Tahiti a multitude of Oceanic art objects as well as a pen name, Loti, after one of his heroes. In 1877, on his return from an initial sojourn in Istanbul, he began work on a "Turkish Salon," incorporating a stucco ceiling inspired by Grenada's Alhambra and North African ceramics, and decked out with carpets, wall-hangings, and striped cushions. Little bothered with stylistic authenticity, Pierre Loti's idea was to "create an atmosphere," choosing each element above all for its emotive value and evocative power.

To the "Turkish Salon," and in the same Orientalist vein that had become so voguish in the nineteenth century but which was rarely as successfully carried off as here, Loti later added an "Arab Chamber" and a mosque, the most spectacular room in the house, with fountain, columns, marble inlay, ceramics, and a positively Thousand-and-One-Nights decor. The cherry on the cake was the opera-buffa minaret, erected in 1907.

Such intense activity would have burnt out, or at least ruined, a lesser man, but, thanks to such works as *Aziyadé*, *The Romance of a Spahi*, *My Brother Yves*, and *Madame Chrysanthemum*, the author earned an income comparable to our own literary highfliers. An unflagging worker, fascinated by foreign climes and peoples, and obsessive about the past, Loti appears to have been insatiable. Concocting an exoticism to his own, very personal, taste, and sparing no expense in the process, Loti was unconcerned with the strict interpretation of historical styles.

A gigantic Renaissance hall, complete with Flemish tapestries and coffered ceiling, for instance, gave him ample scope to satisfy his aristocratic pretensions. He dreamt up a coat-of-arms which he had engraved on stained glass and crowned by his motto: *mon mal m'enchante* ("my misfortune delights me")! In this hall, our miracle-worker threw the most opulent parties: sometimes as many as two hundred guests would climb the asymmetric flights of the monumental stairway. The most memorable occasion, a Louis XI dinner, took place in the Gothic hall, where the ornately carved stall backs, the enormous fireplace and the shelves weighed down by chalices played host to nightly visitors and delusions of grandeur alike.

But all his follies, wanderings, and amorous conquests did not prevent Loti from becoming an exemplary husband and father. His mother, often enlisted to hem the threadbare silks or to ruche the curtains, played along with her son's fantasies. Her stamp is visible in the velvet-hung Red Salon, with its Louis XVI commode, its

In the middle of the house stands the Renaissance Hall in which the coffered ceiling and huge fireplace proclaim Loti's status as a highly successful author. Used in the past as a reception room, its walls are hung with five precious seventeenth-century Flemish tapestries. A stairway leads to the tribune projecting above. Of more modest proportions, the Blue Salon is furnished with eighteenth-century pieces. ABOVE: rich in trees and flowers, the little garden is laid out in a Romantic style.

armchairs, piano, and portraits. The Blue Salon, dedicated to Loti's wife, was complete with pendant tiered chandelier, half-moon console-table and medallion chairs—the aristocratic decor that Blanche, married in 1886, *née* France de Ferrière, might have expected. Figures of Victory decorated the walls of the so-called "Bee" master bedroom, where the keynote is Empire Style.

Tucked away in the center of this maze of add-ons and enlargements whose plan brings to mind a Chinese puzzle, there nestles Loti's private chamber. Standing at the end of a dark corridor, it is a narrow, whitewashed room, with an iron bedstead, a crucifix, a Buddha, and a copy of the Qu'ran co-existing in a forward-looking form of ecumenism. Did Pierre Loti, immune to such talismans, die godless, as he feared he might? This is another secret Loti took with him to the grave. Today, one can visit the house still haunted by his spirit. It served but as the backdrop to a life that was worth at least three: a life divided between the sea, the land, and the clouds beyond.

ANDREW LOGAN

Color on High

"*I* enjoy it so much here that I never really want to go out," Andrew Logan declares. "Here" is in the heart of Bermondsey, London, in a house designed for him by his architect friend Michael Davis to house his extravagant sculptures and provide an ideal space for creative work. Andrew possessed a vital need for color and space. Michael understands this all too well: he feels the same way. To contrast with the ambient gray, he thus chose strong colors—pink, blue, yellow, green, red—and, like Luis Barragán, the Mexican architect whom he considers as his mentor, set them in broad sweeps over the walls. A single hue per room, perhaps two. Not counting the additional notes of color in the furnishings, carpets, pictures, or flowers. Such daring has paid off handsomely.

But, guts alone could never have transformed an old garage, squashed in between a soup-kitchen and a ramshackle pub, into an extravagant aerial space: impudent architectural prowess relies on perfect mastery of volume and material.

Michael and Andrew bought this place at the end of the 1980s—their previous address was the top of a building over a disused cinema. There too, they lived "under glass." When they were dislodged to make room for its renovation, they scoured the land for something similar, but couldn't find it. Let's build our own, they thought. The result is the spectacular glass roof over the toyland maisonnette à la *Belle de Cadiz* housing the bedrooms and bathroom. The rest of the impressively vast floor area is invaded by Andrew's works, including an immense Pegasus whose huge wings are studded with mirror-glass, an unusual technique that resurfaces in the baroque jewelry that has earned him the nickname, "the contemporary Fabergé." Such flattering comparisons do not turn Mr. Logan's head, however.

The room that Andrew Logan uses as a studio possesses a triangular glass roof
that covers the little "Spanish" house. Michael Davis has used the same type of pink paint
as Ludwig II of Bavaria chose for his palaces.

Andrew Logan sitting in front of one of his outlandish sculptures.
RIGHT: a collection of photos and portraits of friends

adorns the yellow walls of the bedroom. Throw with Turkish stripes.
FACING PAGE: the generously proportioned blue room on the first floor doubles as library, kitchen, and dining room.

Such a weighty crown does not bother him. He is determined to wear more than one hat (or peaked cap) in life, and orchestrate events, organize exhibitions, or kick-start parties. A ubiquitous showbiz personality, it was as "Host and Hostess" at a send-up beauty pageant, the "Alternative Miss World," that a ballgown-bedecked Andrew made his first star appearance on the London stage. He has no regrets about an ambivalent, if entirely fitting, debut that has stuck to him. It's simply one role among many.

Less exuberant than his partner, Michael Davis has chosen color and form as his modes of expression. The orange façade like a giant screen opening on to the street turns the head of more than one passer-by. They stop in their tracks. And listen. They'd like to know what is all means. Outlandish lives must unfold behind such a front door, with its bright blue frame. Movie-star destinies? Beyond the door, you do indeed enter a Technicolor universe. The large room that serves as both kitchen and office on the ground floor is blue, the yellow bedroom leads to an emerald green bathroom, and, when Andrew makes an appearance on the little house's pink balcony, he's definitely not sporting a gray business suit. As for alabaster, marble, granite, he's left them to other hands. Resin, mirror-glass, precious or semi-precious stones are his forte, and he's been working with them with diabolical virtuosity for thirty years. It is no surprise then to find Elton John, Koo Stark, Anita Pallenberg among his groupies, all of whom could be said to have affinities with the Angel of the Bizarre. More unexpected is to note the name of Queen Elizabeth the Queen Mother among the list of his collectors. Andrew Logan's celebrity long ago extended beyond the intimate circle of "the people."

At the moment, a sizeable commission lies on the drawing-board: a seven-meter high golden Pegasus destined to fly off to somewhere in the Midlands.

The Lalannes

The House of Inspiration

The Poet and his Muse. The painter and his model. Ideal couples we know well: the cliché, "woman counts on man to ensure her posterity" (or at least to ensure a good life) is a hardy perennial. Since Pygmalion, the roles have altered somewhat: producer and actress, choreographer and ballerina, conductor and star soloist. There too, examples are legion and, if it's true that in this way everyone knows their place ("her" for a start), then at least everyone is happy ("him" for one).

In the world of the creator and the created, the Lalannes present quite a different proposition: two genuine creatives, who since they first met in 1952, have lived together, worked side by side, and enjoyed parallel, independent, yet equally successful careers.

In 1967, they found a house where they could put down some roots. In Ury, near Fontainebleau: a house with two or three centuries on the clock, but which, cherished and lived in as it has always been, doesn't look its age.

You enter it across a paved courtyard where you can stroke a donkey, count the sheep, pat a cow or two, or, more bizarrely, wish good morning to a hippo, or stumble across a wild boar. This bestiary in bronze is by François-Xavier. Just a sample of his work, however, other examples stand out of harm's way in rows in a shed, while the largest individuals, indifferent to rain and gale, are dotted about in the adjoining woods.

They are visible from the house, a kind of Noah's Ark that has been invaded by Claude's vegetal sculpture. She molds anything and everything that takes her fancy: flowers, fruit, leaves, but also a hand, or a pair of lips, casting and carving them in copper or bronze. After numerous experiments, she adopted the electroplating

The living room: the fireplace and all the animals
—except for the little dog lying on the rug—
were made by the master of the house.

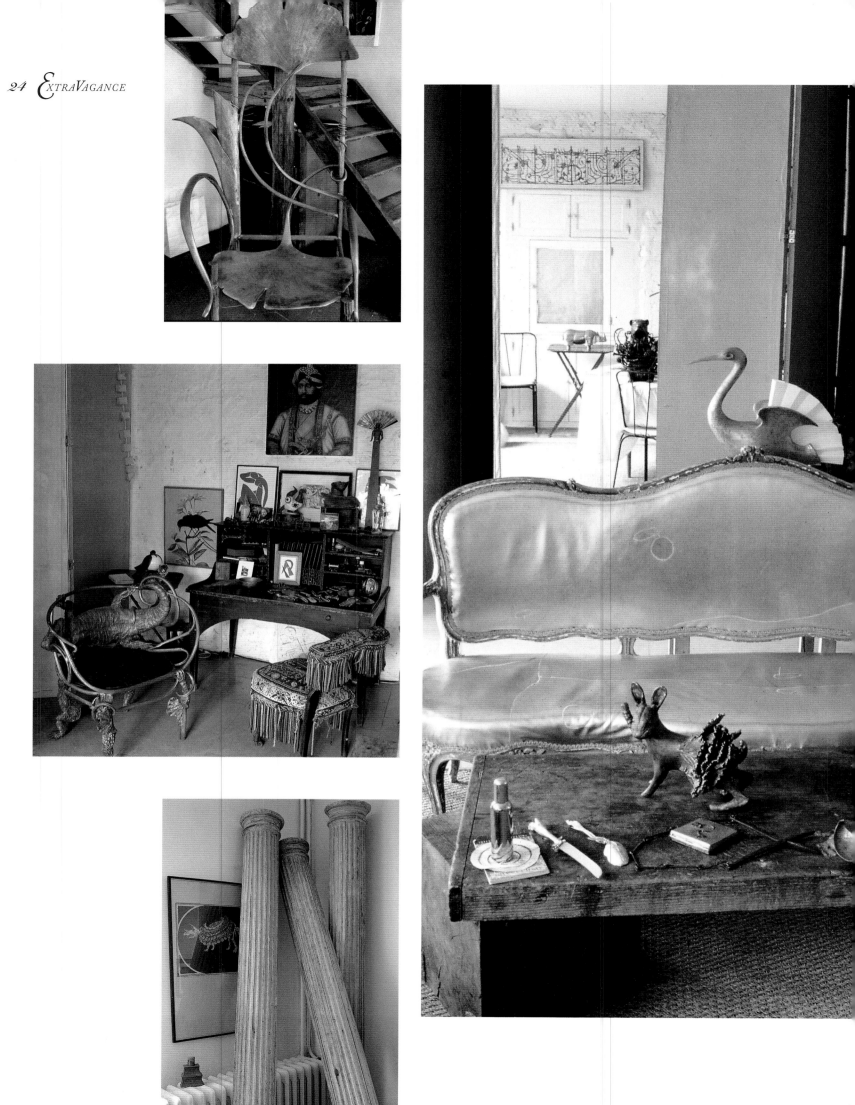

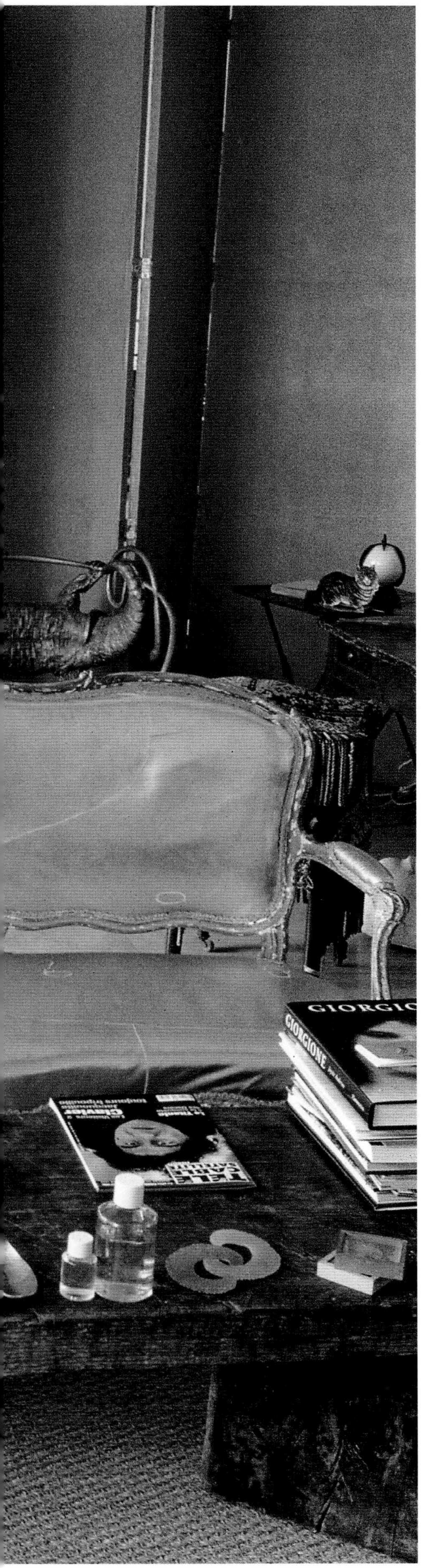

techniques used by silversmiths. At the request of Yves Saint-Laurent in 1969, she cast the bust of Verushka (the "Claudia Schiffer" of the time), the glistening breastplate being used as the bustier for a priceless evening dress. She has also designed jewelry in a poetic vein, "Objets du Désir," produced by Artcurial. But, though the Lalannes have always been courted by fashion, they keep their distance. Otherwise, what with the whirl of collections here, and first nights and thrashes there, they would never have had enough energy to throw themselves into a re-creation of the world, to make one better than the first time. They would never have had the time to dream up their magnificent zoo which, in 1998, transformed the parc de Bagatelle into a second Garden of Eden. Their retrospective, organized under the auspices of the City of Paris, showed how the Lalannes, bought by the greatest collectors and exhibited in the most prestigious museums, delight all those who see their work, from children dragged to the show by their parents to weekenders out for a breath of fresh air. Their art speaks as much to the heart as to the eye, in a language everyone can understand, without having to decode it or puzzle about its cultural references. In Japan, the Lalannes were enshrined as "Living Treasures." In France, they are revered and admired, but they are left quietly alone to live the life of constant work, of ceaseless experiment, they have chosen. In her own private hideaway, a greenhouse in the garden, Claude lets her baroque-leaning inspiration take her wherever it wants. Without preparatory sketches, she dreams accessories in the form of pampas grass or buttercups, or extravagant silver-gilt cutlery whose handles combine dragonfly wings and orchid petals. But also curious creatures like the "Cabbage-Head Man" bought by the singer Serge Gainsbourg, who dedicated a track to her, or madcap furniture, like the armchair with monkeys scrambling down creepers or the console-table draped in an electroplated crocodile skin.

In a nearby workshop, the craftsman François-Xavier miraculously creates and solders large, placid animals. Far removed from all the "-isms" of Paris, their smooth, rounded forms follow the tradition of Pompon and Brancusi, but infused with François-Xavier's own personal brand of humor. As he explains: "Art has been oversacralized in the West, the ancients only thought of art in respect to its usefulness."

Objects by Claude Lalanne on an untreated wood table standing before a Louis XV banquette upholstered in silvered leather. The gingko-leaf armchair is also by her, as is the crocodile chair in front of the small period desk, both in bronze. In the entrance hall, three timber columns in front of a Max Ernst lithograph.

People have boring interiors, and there's no need for it, artists don't need to be like that." So, this particular Trojan Horse brings into the house a "toad" easy-chair, a "donkey-back" desk, a "pigeon" lamp, or a "hippo" bath so as to undermine his sworn enemies, earnestness and pomposity. You can use them, you can smile at them, you can feel for them. At Ury, the metallic masterpieces can enjoy the company of dogs, cats, and birds that wander about freely, inside and out.

In the house, the kitchen comes first. A genuine farmhouse kitchen like any other, but where the sheet-steel extractor-hood was made by the owners. It is in the kitchen that all meals are taken and all friends and family received, including four daughters, one who assists her mother, and, of course, grandchildren. Then you go from a dining room, whose circular table serves as a desk most of the time, into a living room bisected by a big folding screen. You settle down on an eighteenth-century banquette upholstered in silvered leather or a simple iron seat, or a bronze throne adorned with ginkgo leaves. The plain wood table, like the little secrétaire, the pinewood sideboard, like in fact every available surface, is covered with objects by either Claude or François-Xavier that demonstrate the union of Nature and Art and celebrate a couple the like of which one encounters all too rarely.

Not only because of what they do, but also because of who they are, the Lalannes could serve to illustrate an essay by the sociologist Irène Pennachioni. After the description of the "nice couple," in which husband and wife, as if they'd just stepped off an advertisement billboard, go together "as the wealthy like to do, just so they don't have to rub shoulders with others," and the "model couple," which embodies "a signed and delivered contract that stipulates time and timetable," Pennachioni then stresses the scarcity of what she calls the "beautiful couple," one which carries within it both a "love story lived through together, and a vision of complementary harmony."

The Lalannes form just such a "beautiful couple."

A whole bestiary in bronze lives in the small woods behind the house. The carp and the duck are by François–Xavier, the little girl with the hen, by Claude. Back in the house, in front of the window, Sèvres porcelain ostriches by François–Xavier. The artist is often to be seen drawing on the garden table in the living room. The copper and bronze chandelier is by Claude.

Deyan Sudjic created most of his 1970s lofts in industrial spaces or craft shops: warehouses, storefronts, print shops, abandoned factories. Descendants of artist's studios, especially of nineteenth-century examples where academic painters would unroll their interminable canvases, lofts in New York, London, and Paris initially attracted painters, photographers, architects, and designers. These recycle-friendly locales stood in cheap and cheerful, unfashionable districts, and seemed perfectly adapted to the new demands: a thirst for space, the possibility of molding the available volumes to suit the moment, a will to preserve the historic urban fabric, a desire to unite private and professional life under one roof.

The media spotlight was turned on the trend by Andy Warhol and his famous Factory. Soon on both sides of the Atlantic—inevitably a decade later in Europe—the loft became a fashion phenomenon. In Paris, various trendies (stylists, creatives, advertising execs, filmmakers, showbiz folk generally) just had to have one, just as they needed the rough-stone farmhouse in the Lubéron and the beachfront on the Île de Ré. But there were never going to be enough lofts to go around. To satisfy their customers, certain unscrupulous interior decorators started revamping (read, in some cases, destroying) beautifully proportioned five-room apartments on Baron Haussman's boulevards by knocking through partition-walls, stripping off moldings, and tearing out built-in gilt-frame mirror overmantels. A similar, frankly surgical, operation was planned by a journalist, Deyan Sudjic, in London at the beginning of the 1980s.

The apartment was formed originally by the amalgamation of two contiguous floors in a pair of buildings dated 1840. The new owner had previously lived in a

The two apartments on the same floor
are connected by an opening
in the form of an outsized keyhole.

The various spaces are separated by aluminum sheeting.
Furniture has been kept to a strict minimum:
the Rietveld red-and-black armchair at the foot of the bed and,
in the "living room," an Italian sofa, and a coffee table.

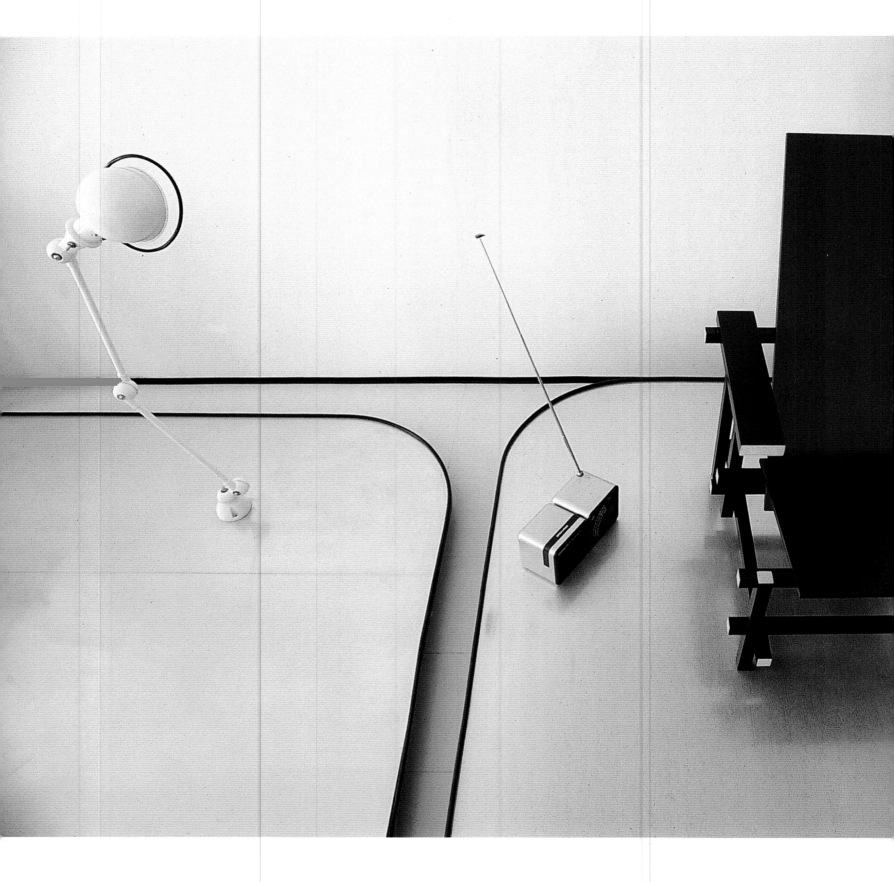

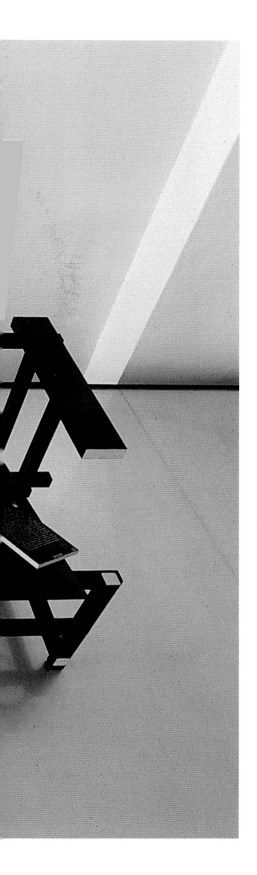

loft which he didn't much care for: too dark. So he commissioned two architects from the Future Systems agency, David Nixon and Jan Kaplicky, to realize his dreams: more air, more light, more sunshine!

Lofts have always provided architects with ideal spaces in which to experiment, whether testing untried materials or solving new problems. Having worked with Richard Rogers and Norman Foster, enthusiasm was all the greater on Jan Kaplicky's side since he'd just been awarded the research account for the interior of NASA's space capsules.

After six months' building work, Deyan Sudjic was flying around in his very own space capsule, but without leaving the stratosphere. The many partitions had been removed and the floating floors delimited various zones of the apartment according to function. Concealed beneath the aluminum cladding, the electric circuits were so arranged that one could plug the lights straight in. From the living room you make your way through a gigantic keyhole-shaped opening to the dining room, moving from one building to the next as from the Victorian era to the Space Age.

Though not of the same dimensions, and designed with a different purpose in mind, this interior was very much in the original spirit of a "traditional" loft. If the result, though audacious, has not earned universal acclaim, nonetheless, just like Sudjic, we all want to be left to adapt our living space to our every whim.

BEAUTIFULLY WAXED PIECES HIDDEN AWAY IN
AN ORDINARY-LOOKING NEW YORK BUILDING BY
AN EXTRAORDINARY COLLECTOR

Waxing Lyrical

George Way was not born with a silver spoon in his mouth. This may account for the pride with which he shows the one he bought for a few dollars at a flea market. Signed Jesse Kip, its twin, which lives in the Metropolitan Museum, is today worth a mint. Unlike the wealthy who often know nothing, collect because it's the thing to do, fall easy prey for dealers, and are fleeced by consultants who charge them the earth, George Way did it all the hard way, clambering up the slippery slope that leads from untutored amateur to all-knowing professional unaided.

It all began quite by chance. Just like in those epic love stories where a glance stolen between two people who don't know each other throws their lives and those closest to them into chaos. Less romantically and less tragically, George found his vocation after an encounter with a button. His whole life was changed by the copper specimen he picked up on the street at Valley Forge in Pennsylvania, at George Washington's summer encampment where (the other) George was spending his long vacation. He took it to the local museum where it was identified: it came off a uniform dating from the Civil War. The wardens thought the kid's behavior rather striking, so they took him round the museum letting him have a look at the things that interested him, telling him where they came from, and how much they were worth. George got the bug. Today the infection is so serious that he is treated by experts as one of their own, a genuine connoisseur. He also numbers among the hundred greatest collectors in all the United States and the lectures he gives to investors in New York are packed to the rafters. There, he helps people spend the sort of money that he for one has never had. He earned his every dollar by the sweat of his brow, working day in, day out in his grocery store, scraping enough money

In the living room, the furniture is of solid oak, the many pictures worthy
of a great museum, the majority being English and Dutch portraits
from the seventeenth and eighteenth centuries.

George Way works on a table from the seventeenth century. Indeed, nearly all the furniture dates from this period. The carved wood bed is, however, Elizabethan. Like all the larger pieces of the time, it comes apart to make transportation easier. ABOVE: One of the high points of the George Way collection, believed to be a self-portrait by the twenty-five-year-old Rembrandt.

together to buy antiquities, hunting them down, restoring them, and preserving them.

If he'd only sold off a piece or two every now and again, George could have retired ages ago, but it's something that's never even entered his head, and so he carries on in business regardless. He has no desire to travel, says he doesn't bother with clothes much, but is careful to finish work early.

By late afternoon, George is to be found in his three-room apartment in an unprepossessing New York building. A faint light dodges in between heavy velvet curtains, and it is in this thoughtful, almost religious, atmosphere that George practices his own personal ancestor cult. A hundred or so sixteenth- and seventeenth-century portraits. Silverware, with German and English furniture of the same period. Chairs, tables, chests of drawers, often of vast size, have taken the place over to the extent that it is no easy task to beat a way through. Nonetheless, our friend can enjoy sleeping in a huge four-poster that required the combined efforts of nine men to move it in.

If fire broke out in his home, what would he grab first? George Way rejects the idea out of hand. We can imagine him sitting tight or, if pulled struggling from the burning pile, being consumed with grief. No such terror lurks on the horizon, however, so the question simply hangs in the air, unanswered. He leaves one clue, however. In New York very few people know what solid oak is, he tells us sadly as he lovingly passes a hand over a bust of Charles I carved out of his favorite wood. It is his opinion that the best way of gauging the quality of a piece, of judging how it is built, of appreciating its details is to wax it, to make it shine. This is a task George delegates to no one. And when he lays down the dust cloth, it is only to take up the pen. He has his own column in a newspaper and is preparing a book designed for the edification of the average American reader, a person who generally thinks antiques are "old stuff" and often can't tell rosewood from mahogany.

His dream? That his collections will one day be housed in a museum bearing his name.

The Art of Happiness

What's the connection between Ludwig II of Bavaria and a Barbie Doll? Renoir and a supermarket calendar? Buddha and John Travolta? Shocking pink and rose-tinted spectacles? Pierre et Gilles, who've taken an opt-out on choosing. And, while they've been busy with everything and everyone they've taken a fancy to—or simply fancied—mixing it nicely and serving it shaken in a little side street on the Pré Saint Gervais, out in the 'burbs, they've also been creating themselves a decor that fits their work to a "T." As overstocked as the gift department in the run-up to Christmas, souvenirs and fun things scale the walls and scuttle over the shelving: cheapo knick-knacks brought back from every corner of the globe—souks in Marrakech, bazaars in India, street markets in Mexico—arranged in a stage set to their own design, as they chat about the lighting, the backdrops, the accessories, the costumes—and the make-up.

Pierre and Gilles have been inseparable since they first met at a party at Kenzo's in 1976 which they left on the same scooter. Complementing each other perfectly, the two originals still live and work together. Pierre, who studied photography in Geneva, prints up the pictures of the chosen few in the basement of an apartment that doubles as a film studio. Then Gilles, who went through Beaux-Arts and started out as an illustrator, painstakingly reworks, retouches, and repaints the photo so that every defect, every untimely effect, is eradicated. Here, the artificial is not kept under wraps—it flaunts itself for all to see.

Their sitters? Actresses, singers, models who can see themselves portrayed as pretty-pretty fairy princesses or as butter-wouldn't-melt-in-her-mouth Madonnas, and laugh: Lio, Sylvie Vartan, Claudia Schiffer, Nina Hagen, Arielle Dombasle, among others. But there is a fair sprinkling of blond boyz too, half innocent, half

The heavily ornamented spiral staircase connects a pair of bedrooms above to a basement

room equipped as a film studio for Pierre and Gilles to stage their artworks in.

FOLLOWING PAGES: the kitchen, as "dressy" as any living room. The mosaic walls are lined with kitsch.

provocative, and every man jack of them gay, but gay in trumps. For even if it's never been the be all and end all of their business, homosexuality has always been essential to Pierre et Gilles' erotic and poetical world.

Hence their series of portraits of "Pretty Thugs" and "Little Boxers," but also "Saints," the "Shipwrecked," and those they sent to "La Beauté en Avignon," the showcase exhibition of the year 2000, "Rhoda" (gender?) and "Krishna" (gender?), as androgynous as you like and enthusiastically received by the chief curator of the show, Jean de Loisy. " Pierre et Gilles' photos make it seem like our dreams have come true."

Though skilled in the use of creamy pastel, in starry starry nights and in golden draperies, and though mad about the slicked-back heroes of India's Bollywood cinema, Pierre et Gilles see red when their style is described as "kitsch." We find in their work, however, all the characteristics of the genre listed by a theoretician such as Abraham Moles, who dubs kitsch the "art of a happiness": surfaces brimful of

over-decorated objects; plastic flowers; fairy lights; materials that mimic other materials; mock wood, fake marble, mock fake phony everything. It's enough to give a functionalist a heart attack, and a minimalist, heartburn.

But, if not everyone succumbs to the temptation of the "social acceptability of pleasure by secret communication in the idiom of an undemanding and moderate bad taste," as kitsch is described by Mr. Moles, there is somewhere lurking in all of us a kitsch tendency just itching to get out. That Pierre et Gilles feign ignorance—or exploit it—is their own business. And it's a business that's doing well. After conquering the United States with a retrospective at the New Museum, New York, their exhibition at the FIAC 2000 with the Galerie Jérôme de Noirmont swept all before them.

Two hundred years ago, Hegel described art as the "highest joy man can give himself." With two heads for such dizzy heights, Pierre et Gilles are enjoying the climb.

The television proudly sits atop a mosaic stand in the shape of a temple. The doll and the "blackamoor" are in the living room.
Placed upon a wrought iron armchair, a photo of French singing star Sylvie Vartan printed on to a cushion.
Behind, an Indian flute player, highly representative of the interior decor.
FAR LEFT: Pierre (with brown hair) and Gilles (seated) having coffee.

Flights of Fancy

" *M* y imagination will live on after me," Piero Fornasetti foretold. And so it has come to pass, as long as his son Barnaba persists in dancing in his father's footsteps. Instead of grumbling on in the way of sons of famous men, condemned, as they put it, to eke out a life in the shadow of their genial forebears, he has blossomed, with his beautiful American wife, Betony, a jewelry designer, and with his children, in what Ettore Sottass has admiringly described as a "marvelous world of images and fragments, quotations, and memory." It even seems natural that Barnaba Fornasetti lives with his family under the paternal roof in a wing of the house in Milan, where he has set up studio and offices. There, while carefully tending the ten thousand or so pieces created by his father, he continues to enrich and diversify a wide-ranging collection that goes from dinner services to furniture, from fabrics to ceramics, from lamps to wallpaper.

Piero Fornasetti, who began designing when he was ten and only stopped on 15 October 1988, the day he died, once confessed: "I use everything—glass, metal, marble—but everything I can get my hands on." Taking his inspiration from Palladian architects and Piranesi's dizzying perspectives, he found his own personal style almost immediately. In their rectangular geometry, the furniture he designed together with Gio Ponti in the 1950s, the bureaus, writing-tables, chests of drawers, etc., squarely resemble monumental sculptures. No trompe-l'oeil is involved, however: a virtuoso in changing scale, in transforming volumes into flat surfaces, Fornasetti did not want to deceive the eye, but to discompose the mind.

Architectural motifs reappear on scarves and dinner plates. One of his fetishes for example is the obelisk; but there are others, the sun, the hand, the playing card, and a mysterious female face in no less than five hundred versions. Whenever

With Fornasetti, everything begins with drawing and ends with the art of the antique.

In the office, large screenprint canvases act as sliding partitions.

In front, a "Balloon" chair in lacquered wood.

Fornasetti chose a theme, he exploited it doggedly, reproducing it tirelessly in hundreds of variations, every one different.

Considered today as a master of twentieth-century decorative arts—and Patrick Mauriès' important study (Thames & Hudson, London) is well worth reading in this connection—at the height of his fame, Fornasetti worked with no less than thirty collaborators. In the 1970s, however, he could observe, no doubt with a hint of bitterness, his star beginning to wane. But by the 1980s, a growing taste for the 1950s won him a second spring of the sort few artists live to enjoy. With fresh energy, and aided and abetted by his son Barnaba, he started designing anew and producing editions of earlier pieces. They turned up in Milan, in Turin, even in Paris, at L'Éclaireur. Some pieces of furniture cost a small fortune, but it is possible to buy oneself a lamp, a teapot, or a tray without breaking the bank, and compose a carefully selected anthology of these antique fragments built into something fresh by a fertile imagination.

Barnaba hardly had the choice: he lives and breathes the Fornasetti world. This is no mausoleum though; in the office, you work beneath vast silkscreen prints, you eat in the dining room seated on sun-drenched chairs, take your shower in a room lined with "Bibliothèque" tiles, and sip your coffee in an everyday-looking service whose porcelain (the style lifted from newspaper layout) reminds one of Fornasetti's passion for graphic art. His preference for black and white was a necessary consequence of this love of printing. The only touches of color in the Milan apartment come from Betony—a matching chair, the back wrapped in a turban in the Venetian manner. At the Fornasetti's, the supreme luxuries, even art itself, are something you can sit on.

All the furniture was made by the Master who was responsible for designing thousands of items.
LEFT: a "Sun" ceiling lamp and a chest of drawers. In the bedroom: the period bed draped
in a patterned fabric. ABOVE: Barnaba Fornasetti, the son of Piero, with his wife Betony, a jewelry
designer. The ceramic breakfast table is printed with a newspaper motif.

The Stuff That Dreams Are Made Of

*P*aul Jones is possessed by an absolute passion for fabric. And, as he is also a dyed-in-the-wool interior designer, he has naturally turned his little three-bedroom apartment in Soho, London, into a bolt-hole for the velvets, damasks, tartans, and other textiles he hunts for far and wide, piling them up and combining them with frenetic abandon.

For mere mortals, such a riot of color would seem to call for a neutral backdrop, but Paul finds neutral boring, and boredom is his sworn enemy. That's where his accomplice, the painter Tom Hammond, comes into his own. Except for the strictly functional kitchen and bathroom, nothing remains untouched by his brush. In the blue living room, for instance, Tom began by attacking the ceiling. Tiny cupids dart in and out of the trelliswork, while leaves float down, showering the newly gold-painted concrete flooring. The walls too harmonize with the sumptuous eighteenth-century silk drapes from Lyon. A large mirror perpetrates an act of singular deception: thought up much like a stage set, this baroque interior—or perhaps "boudoir for Dangerous Liaisons" would be more accurate—is in fact no bigger than a box at the opera. Let's hear it for Paul Jones, then, an artist who has had his chairs upholstered in crimson velvet to bring out the armorial bearings and the trimming he adores.

Elsewhere, a scatter of petit-point cushions, a Scots plaid, and a panther skin meet up, as if by chance, on a tiny wrought-iron bed. "Chance" has been given a helping hand, though, since, beginning by selling bolts of cloth on the sidewalk, Paul Jones has never stopped reading and learning, running from museum to auction room, so his "improvisations" are always rooted in a solid cultural awareness.

A feeling for authenticity is not the reason behind his decking out the majestic

A glorious specimen of Paul Jones's taste for bold contrasts:
panther skins, historic tartan, and petit-point cushions cavort together
on a Romantic-style wrought iron bed.

Tom Hammond derived the painted decor in the living room from a bit of dilapidated wall. The Lyon silk curtains are of the same style as the gilded mirrors and chandeliers. ABOVE: the hand of justice, a rococo applique, and a detail of the cupids flying around the ceiling.

branches of a gilt chandelier in candles, however, or, more strangely, for leaving them to burn day and night. Paul hates both natural and electric light in equal measure. One day he closed his shutters forever, and now lives, silk lover that he is, like a worm in a cocoon, behind drawn curtains. In any case, he only comes home at night, while at dawn he's already left to scour the flea-markets, before the long procession of meetings with buyers and clients, in London, or Paris, Rome, and Madrid, just as long as it's a quick return trip: Paul is happiest at home and only sleeps soundly in his own bedroom, whose tone is given by the nineteenth-century Gothic fabric on the valance and the wall-hangings. Tom Hammond for his part has dotted the wall with fleurs-de-lis, turned the plywood flooring into patinated mosaic, and populated the entire space with the kind of monkeys that pop up in eighteenth-century chinoiserie. You enter the noiseless flat down a crimson and gold corridor, and beneath the enigmatic gaze of icons. Outside, there are cars, shop windows, neon lights, crowds, noise.

Which life is real?

The bedroom is decorated with singeries *in a French eighteenth-century style, though the general ambiance is more medieval. The baldachin and the curtains are nineteenth-century fabrics from Lyon in a Neo-Gothic vein. In the corridor the icons and portraits of saints on the red fleur-de-lis ground were also painted by Tom Hammond.* RIGHT: *Paul Jones seated on a pile of cushions.*

MARC-ANDRÉ HUBIN

Looking Back at the 1980s

"*It* is the space within to be lived in (quoting from Lao Tse) not the walls and roofs and floors," Frank Lloyd Wright said of the essence of architecture. In *The Natural House* (1954), the American architect went on to note that "when the house-interior absorbs the chair in perfect harmony then we will have achieved . . . a culture of our own."

A half-century later, be it through lack of funds or of rigor, his call for "a perfect harmony" has hardly been answered. The interior designed, decorated, and furnished by Gaëtano Pesce is thus all the more remarkable. It did not survive its original owner who passed away prematurely and only photographs remain as evidence of what audacious taste can do when seconded by great wealth.

In the mid-1980s, a young photographer, Marc-André Hubin, acquired a 200m^2 apartment on avenue Foch. He possessed some fine 1950s pieces and collected Carlo Mollino furniture, but had no desire to live in a museum. In those days, no queues snaked around the Louvre. People preferred to hang out in galleries, stores, cafes, at parties. The "Society of Spectacle" was in full swing. A tidal wave of "images" orchestrated by "creatives"—designers, filmmakers, photographers— flooded the media, poured into the street. "Memphis" guru Ettore Sottsass was all enthusiasm. "Our terror of the past has evaporated—we can now go forward with a light heart." OK, let's go, Marc-André Hubin said to himself and bought an extraordinary table in Milan: the top covered by a red, green, and white plastic puddle, supported by four feet that don't seem quite to keep up which each other. Cassina, who exhibited the prototype, introduced him to its creator. Everything stemmed from this first crucial meeting: carte blanche, with a blank check to match, and Gaëtano Pesce was hired to refurbish the entire avenue Foch triplex.

Through a rectangular opening in the wall one can glimpse the bedroom, framed like a picture. Above the bed with its duvet, a giant clock. A steel garage door serves as a partition between bedroom and living room.

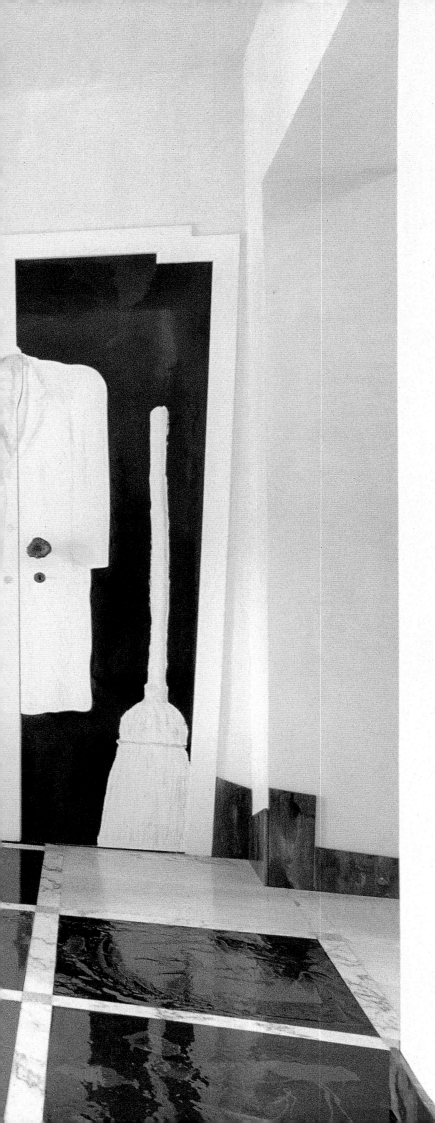

Devising original solutions for each new space, Gaëtano Pesce oversaw the whole project from conception to execution. LEFT: stretches of wall in the hall "distressed" and varnished black. The flooring consists of resin tiles, each with a different decor. ABOVE: a hand-shaped door. TOP: a resin table with asymmetrical feet produced by Cassina.

A leading theoretician of "alternative" design and a sworn enemy of the reductive rationalism of the 1960s and of mass production, whose dully repetitive character he lambasted, Pesce was a fierce advocate of "variety," that he championed as being "vital to life." One could never accuse this intrepid explorer of new technologies, forms, and materials of living in the misty-eyed past, however. His agenda was to rid us of the universal and bring in the individual, to once again make emotion integral to creativity.

The site Hubin entrusted to Pesce provided a unique opportunity to let his provocative architectural talents off the leash and to put into practice the theories he had already been teaching in Strasbourg, Milan, São Paulo, and New York, his chosen residence since 1983.

In 1987, after two years work, Marc-André Hubin was at last able to sit down on the furniture Pesce had specially designed for him, which was produced in Venice (where Pesce had earlier studied), and to contemplate the marvelously limber curves of his Carlo Mollino collection. The most astounding, most extravagant, thing, however, was the theatrical way the whole space was organized. The huge mantelpiece, beneath which flames leapt in a fireplace

shaped like a giant mask; a door in the form of a hand fashioned by specialist shipbuilders; the walls coated in black varnish and lined in steel and zinc; the bedroom framed by a rectangular aperture above the staircase, cut out like a picture; the irregularly patterned plastic flooring; the library lighting composed of blown-glass spheres, miracles of Venetian artistry, perched atop thin metal poles.

The task of transforming a "de luxe" 1930s-style apartment into a king-size manifesto of visionary design presupposes an exceptional relationship between creator and client. In a story that could have only happened to two very special people, choices, ambitions, and risks all had to be shared equally. Hubin had no scruples when it came to writing the final chapter. *Destroy,* he said.

Overall view of the mezzanine floor opposite the bedroom. An illuminated "balustrade" made of glass spheres perched on flexible steel poles runs round the library.
LEFT: in the living area, a totem-like fireplace resembling a face.
The few pieces of furniture not by Pesce, such as the seats and the tables, are by the great 1940s designer Carlo Mollino, of whose works Marc-André Hubin was a major collector.

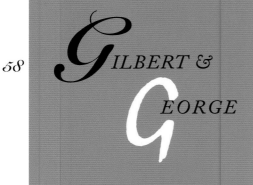

GILBERT AND GEORGE'S QUIET, SUBVERSIVE INTERIOR
IN THEIR LONDON HOUSE

A Two-I'd Team

A singular plural that encompasses an artistic duo that speaks with one voice but signs with a "double-barreled" name. A singular contrast too, between the peaceful environment in which they spend their lives and the subversive goal they have chosen for themselves: to make the images literally scream in the viewer's face, to affect people so that after looking at the pictures, they feel different when they go home.

"Different," that's as may be. But no one can have remained indifferent to the hybrids exhibited in Paris' Musée d'Art Moderne late in 1997. One hundred and twenty pieces that summed up thirty years or so of artistic creativity.

Gilbert and George met in 1967 at St. Martin's School of Art in London where they were both studying sculpture. There they played a waiting game, impatient, as if both felt somehow unfinished, each needing the other so as not to feel alone. Togetherness was best. Are they happy? you ask. Well, rich and famous at any rate. Unmoving. Unavoidable.

Their faces covered in bronze paint, straitjacketed in the suits that were soon to become a uniform, it all began way back in 1969, on the day they climbed onto a podium and began to singsong idiotically, moving in time like a couple of robots. This sketch, Living Sculptures, initially thought up as a performance, was the first step in the completion of what was a grand plan: to become both the subject in and the object of work that would be a hybrid between photography and painting. Not standing in front of the picture, but *being* the picture.

Not a single one of their works hangs in their house on Fournier Street, Spitalfields, one of London's less affluent and more ethnically mixed areas. They

Among other things, Gilbert & George collect late nineteenth-century ceramics,
with a predilection for the outlandish designs of Sir Edmund Elton.
Even the cupboards are overflowing with them.

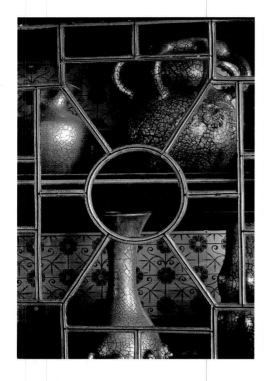

ABOVE: the only contemporary item in the living room, a TV set.

Otherwise all the furnishings, pictures, and objects are period. Gilbert & George particularly like the portrait of a young man (sixteenth century), center, and the Romantic landscape on the left, "the flamboyant ramparts of the world."

began by renting the first floor and brought in two antiquated armchairs, a bed, and a table, before, once they made their fortune, buying up the whole building.

As they say, they are always looking for new ways of manipulating images to make them look stronger, tougher, but also more accessible. They work out of two ultra-modern studios set up behind the house that itself remains much as it was in the eighteenth century when it was occupied by Huguenot refugees. Wood is omnipresent. You can smell it. Gilbert and George patiently rub wax into the wood paneling they stripped themselves. You can hear the wood too, creaking as you mount the stairs.

Their furniture is all solid wood. All in the Arts & Crafts style, imposing, and almost, given the ungenerous size of the rooms, cumbersome. But this is not a place one walks around in: every last inch is crammed with nineteenth-century ceramics and just as many are tidied away in the cupboard. Hundreds of vases come from an eccentric aristocrat, Sir Edmund Elton, while others are signed Christopher Dresser.

On the top floor, there is a living room set aside for gem-encrusted church chandeliers. The few paintings are old too. One modern item: a television. One household

Gilbert & George do not eat at home so the kitchen is devoted to having tea and storing champagne. Like all the other rooms, it has been taken over by books and all kinds of objects. Almost all the dark-wood furniture in house is in the Renaissance-inspired Arts and Crafts.

article: a kettle. Gilbert and George take all their meals at a restaurant, the same one for thirty years, confining their home cooking to tea, (instant) coffee, and champagne. They prefer Ruinart, as much for its name as for its beaded bubbles.

Frozen like in a still life, it would be difficult to imagine a more anachronistic interior for two of the most provocative of contemporary artists. Does it represent their real taste? Or it is their way of swimming against the tide? A carefully staged affair designed to pull the wool over our eyes? Together, all the pictures tell a story, but none can do so alone. One day there will be one final G&G image and then we'll be able to read the whole story. Those left standing will then learn what G&G really stands for.

For more information, read the interview with David Sylvester in the catalog, *Rudimentary Pictures* (Los Angeles/London, 1999).

1980s DESIGNER MARCO DE GUELTZ'S VERY OWN
CRYSTAL PALACE

Through the Looking-Glass

*A*t the beginning of the 1980s, Marco de Gueltz arrived in Paris, and for him his twenties were truly the best years of his life. He'd just returned from a long self-imposed exile in sun-drenched Los Angeles. He'd left his native Roanne with no money and no qualifications to speak of and entered Otis Parson's School. While doing a few odd jobs he thought up the little scheme that was to make his name: he covered T-shirts in resin and sold them as lampshades. It was enlightening. And clever. But fiddly. He abandoned the T-shirt idea pretty quick as he had to buy them in bulk, and moved on to create resin sculptures and light fittings from scratch. His work earned him a debut exhibition in the L. A. Museum of Modern Art and, a bit later, an account that was to thrust him into the spotlight back in Paris: the refurbishment of the Bains Douches night club.

Before starting out on his new path, and before getting into the swing of swinging Paris, Marco de Gueltz had worked in glass. He would recuperate glass from rubbish dumps, then cut, polish, and build it into extravagant assemblages supported or framed in wire. Galleries soon joined the rush, Yves Gastou and Néotu being followed by Les Barbares. Then collectors discovered Marco de Gueltz at shows that resembled poems in glass.

Except for a chair and a chandelier that were brought out in small editions, his creations were always one-offs, expensive certainly, but fabulous. Whereas his contemporaries, Tom Dixon, André Dubreuil, and Mark Brazier-Jones, hit on metal with hammer and anvil, Marco de Gueltz set off to conquer an imaginary realm, guided solely by a lucky star. The Pole Star, or polar at least. The bathroom—hall of mirrors? petrified forest? crystal trap?—testified to his inspiration and its indebtedness to his chosen material.

The bathroom: irregularly shaped panes of reflective glass make for something of a chilly feel.

FOLLOWING PAGES: the stringently designed dining room—whatever's not glass is iron.

The draped silk curtains are the only soft touch.

Glass tables, seats, candelabras, shelving. But also a mantelpiece and a flight of stairs. In the apartment where he lived, quai de Jemmapes, just opposite the Hôtel du Nord, one of the actress Arletty's favorite haunts, the vitreous was everywhere.

And the atmosphere evoked? Fairy tale. Hans Christian Andersen. Except for the bedroom, where theatrical illusion reigned. Unmoving draperies (in plaster) framed the windows. The mirror made the room look double its size. The curtains were a bit of surprise too: real velvet, real color! Marco de Gueltz had little time to sit gazing at them, however. He'd set up a workshop on the ground floor of a disused café that was fit to bursting with projects and unfinished commissions. Some of these were never completed: in 1992, at only thirty-four, the man of glass passed through his transparent world to a more distant shore, more distant even than his dreams.

The fireplace and the standard lamp are by Marco de Gueltz, the paintings and the sculptures by Fabrice Langlade.
Patinated leather easy chairs and sofa.
FACING PAGE: a corner of the dining room. Between the iron-framed mirror and a detail of the table cut out of an acid-treated glass plate, a photograph of Marco de Gueltz.

Creative Salvage

*W*hen, as impoverished young men, André Dubreuil, Mark Brazier-Jones, and Tom Dixon first met in the same down-at-heel London studio, they never dreamt that they were about to write a fresh chapter in the unfolding story of the decorative arts. Dixon least of all. He was the youngest (born in 1959), a self-taught "punk" who had started out, like Ron Arad and the other Brutalists, by giving metal a hard time. His résumé at the time read: "rave organizer." The earliest pieces were constructed out of old ladles, frying pans, and handlebars. These were one-offs that crossbred sculpture and do-it-yourself, marginal hybrids that attracted more than one art gallery. Then, Dixon designed a single, S-line chair, and turned out fifty variants, in rattan, wicker, paper, copper, old tires . . . The firm of Cappellini bought into the model, produced it in editions, and now it has pride of place in every museum on the planet, not least in the Vitra Design Museum, Germany, where, in a building signed Frank Gehry, it nestles beside pieces by Hoffmann, Eames, and Kuramata.

Recycle-man Tom Dixon is now a designer with an international reputation. His furniture is produced by Cappellini (loyalty cuts both ways), his glass pieces by Salviati, his light fixtures by Magis. Two years ago he was chosen as design director for the Habitat Group, with a brief to breathe new life into a store which had long been market leader in a contemporary but realistically affordable style.

He has of course already offered accounts to young designers, such as the Bouroullec brothers and Lisa Norrinder, but the stars for his 2001 collection were first and foremost twentieth-century classics, from Jean Prouvé (1901–1984)

Tom Dixon has installed two steel candlesticks of his own design
on a Boulle–style secrétaire, a family heirloom. A jigsaw-puzzle pattern of slabs
of marble covers the stone-built wall.

General view of the living room. LEFT: around a typical 1960s
glass-topped table, some of Dixon's famous S-line chairs.

to Noguchi (1904–1988), and from Achille Castigliani to Ettore Sottsass—both over eighty themselves. For Dixon, such masters have never been surpassed as regards freedom and modernity.

Whenever he finds the time to build his dream house, at least he'll know where to go to furnish it.

ABOVE: a wrought-iron arabesque and a straw hen found at a flea market; two gold-leafed metal chairs by Dixon. On the 1950s table, an iron cake-dish decorated with cabochons. Finally, Tom Dixon himself in his veteran Jaguar.

73

Arabesques

"Today," as André Dubreuil himself noted, "I'm not rich enough to buy one of my own pieces." Not patient enough either, perhaps: nowadays you don't simply slam the money down for furniture by Dubreuil—you have to order it, wait, and hope. You have to deserve it. And there is *not* enough to go round. Console-table, desk, chest of drawers emerge from the studio at the rate of little more than eight pieces a year. Flanked by half-a-dozen assistants, the craftsman—the artist—now works out of an old sheepcote a few steps from the large family house in the Dordogne countryside to which he retreated ten years ago. Two hours from Paris by high-speed train, he devotes himself to a metier that satisfies him totally but which now takes him over, consuming his life: "Suddenly, I've become stingy with my time." This helps explain his obsession with clocks (he has a collection of more than twenty, caring for them with a vigilant eye) and his decision to remain a bachelor. "I hate timetables, visits, noise—I could never impose my solitude, with no vacations, no entertainment, on anyone else."

Luckily, before becoming famous and off-limits—except if you happen to be Rothschild or Lagerfeld or one of a handful of well-heeled enthusiasts—André Dubreuil did make a few pieces of furniture for himself. He casts his mind back to the time he was living in London and, like Tom Dixon and Mark Jones, discovering the joys of ironwork and welding. This was in the mid-1980s, and he had already had several lives.

On leaving the Inchbald School of Design, he started out as an interior designer. Then turned antiques dealer. He came back from a trip to Italy with a taste for trompe-l'oeil and soon became a virtuoso in the style. Success followed. Orders piled up, but boredom soon set in. His clients all asked for the same things: ruins, colonnades, a Coliseum for the dining-room walls. André had the feeling he was treading water and felt ready for a new challenge. He stumbled upon his new path quite by chance while

The smooth curves of an iron table signed André Dubreuil. One of his earliest pieces standing in front of a replica of Michelangelo's Sybil. Following page: a baroque-style day bed by Mark Brazier-Jones and, to the right, a Tom Dixon side table. The appliques are signed Dubreuil.

giving his pal Tom Dixon a helping hand with a new interior for a teahouse, a future meeting place for hip Londoners. As he watched his friend welding, folding, and bending iron, he made up his mind to try it himself. Head first, he admits—but the ideas flooded in. He knew every furniture style like the back of his hand, could draw from memory every one of Palladio's villas, and already had a personal triumvirate of designers he most admired: Bugatti, Carlo Molino, Gio Ponti. Today, he possesses a selection of their works, no less, but, if Dubreuil's Pantheon is made up of Italian luminaries, he himself is better seen as heir apparent to the great French cabinetmaking tradition. Gazing on a patinated copper chest of drawers, on tables inlaid with mother-of-pearl, or on a rock-crystal sconce, one is reminded above all of marquetry by Boulle and Weisweiler. As for the forms, they hark back to Guimard, Rateau, or Printz, though the materials chosen and the profusion of ornament are Dubreuil's and his alone. As is a recurrent figure in his art, the juxtaposition of full swell and crisp edge. "It's my rendition of Good vs. Evil," he has confessed. It is also surely a way of letting two forms coexist, the sharp stings pricking the heaven-sent curves and preventing them from dropping off to sleep.

Evil, for André Dubreuil, is not only to be found among a long list of crimes—in violence, in war, and in betrayal. It also lurks in fashion, in sheep-like, brain-dead copyists, in idiotic snobbery, in mealy-mouthed arrogance. The same goes for vanity: he never signs his work. Just like the cathedral builders. And, for collectors who might have been thought to voice concern on that account, it matters not a jot. After all, you can tell a Dubreuil at a glance. Even with closed eyes, if you stroke its voluptuous arabesques, its raised inlay. A Dubreuil writing desk or side table is a jewel. Some are in fact incrusted with jade, coral, or pearl.

One day, he'll stop time itself, his old enemy and he'll start making necklaces, bracelets, and rings for the kinds of princesses that no longer exist. Meanwhile, he collects historical armoires, with a preference for examples from Lyon and Bordeaux. And he walks around them. He needs room, and here he can breathe freely. But above all, here he is faced with a project he has cradled through many a sleepless night. In the wardrobe, an unloved if elder son of the furniture world, mistreated for three centuries or more, Dubreuil has found a challenge worthy of his efforts. But he hasn't yet found the material he needs: fascinated by trees, he has never sought to work in wood.

Beneath the photograph of André Dubreuil, an Italian table with a 1950s Vallauris vase and a Mark Brazier-Jones chair. The copper armoire is by Dubreuil himself. FACING PAGE: all the furniture in the kitchen, except for the Brazier-Jones table and chair, is by Dubreuil.

Mark Brazier-Jones

The Wings of Design

*I*f his name is not well-known to the general public it is only because Mark Brazier-Jones is what you'd call an uncommon artist. In every way. He leaves his house deep in the English country only rarely, and with a heavy heart, solely to attend the opening of an exhibition of his work in cities like London, New York, Berlin, Brussels, Tokyo or, as is the case in late 2001, in Paris, at the Avant-Scène gallery. Economical with his talent, only a trickle of pieces ever leave his workshop, each evocative of vanished worlds, of a lost universe of myths and symbols. It is a timeless world that resists the passing of the years, but calls for infinite patience on all sides. Expectation is of course part and parcel of the pleasure: no customer, no matter how jittery or fickle, is going to turn down a piece that's been dreamed of for years. For the meticulous, perfectionist Mark Brazier-Jones, patience itself is a raw material on a par with the bronze and steel with which he has been scrapping for nearly fifteen years.

When, together with Tom Dixon in 1984, Brazier-Jones founded Creative Salvage, a neo-baroque group that went in for cutting, welding, and hammering in a post-punk style, the joy of consumerism was already beginning to pall. As art director for TV shows and rock videos, he benefited from massive budgets and huge teams. He has lost nothing of his sure-fire professionalism, but his abiding memory is of unremitting frustration, since, by his own admission, the majority of the sets he designed either went by in a flash, or, worse still, ended up on the cutting-room floor. Not exactly a career with much of a future.

With scarcely a backward glance, Brazier-Jones left the world of show-stopping and showboating and headed off to a rustic and Arcadian retreat—though it is not quite love in a cottage since the house he and his companion Liza have

On the "pumpkin" table, a still-life composed as a "vanity" and the famous "Olympia" candlesticks crowned with laurel. Animal figures form the legs of the easy chair.

chosen to live in is enormous. From Liza he took the "Brazier" that he has inserted in his original name, an affectionate collage, which, like a tattoo, will never leave him. What does he still need to be really happy? The sea, he says, the sea that rocked him gently when a child in New Zealand, the inspiration, perhaps, behind the fish-shaped candlesticks and "tentacle" feet of certain tables. Other tables, though, have griffin feet, while chair backs can be in the shape of wings or lyres, and wall lights crowned with laurel. It would indeed seem that Mark Brazier-Jones finds more to inspire him in myth than in his immediate environment. Produced in very small runs, his creations are half design and half sculpture and remain the preserve of the chosen few. Very few at all are stored in the house. He has taken his baroque-looking day bed—the same that he made for Dubreuil—with him wherever he lands, however, just like the pumpkin-table made in homage to Cinderella. Without being overly concerned with ornamentation, he is fond of color (there is not a single white wall in the pink house, and the shutters are blue), and chooses precious fabrics for upholstering the chairs, as much for nuances in color as for their feel. Light, which he only likes filtered, is locked up in prismatic globes, and, though he has designed many outlandish chandeliers, he never lets illumination flood an entire room and never forgets to leave enough space for shadow.

And, for fire too. Far from the lamps, it burns away in the fireplace, an indispensable helpmeet to man—and to the creative spirit above all. "To forget to dream before the fireside," Gaston Bachelard reminds us, "is to lose the primal, the truly human use of fire." Mark Brazier-Jones, a burning spirit if ever there was one, has never lost it.

FACING PAGE: André Dubreuil so liked this baroque day bed by Mark Brazier-Jones, that he ordered the same model for himself. Early on the two friends shared studio space with Tom Dixon. ABOVE: The entrance to the house of Mark Brazier-Jones; a photograph of the artist in his studio; and on a table, a few glass pieces from his collection.

Vanessa's Revenge or Return to Charleston

For many years, the talent of the painter and designer Vanessa Bell was somewhat eclipsed by that of her sister, novelist Virginia Woolf. On the occasion of the 1999 Bloomsbury Group exhibition at the Tate Gallery, the balance was at least partially redressed, in the process shedding considerable light on the personality of its central figure. Today, Vanessa's country house of Charleston has become a place of pilgrimage to all those interested in the Bloomsbury style.

It was Virginia who stumbled across what was then an abandoned farmhouse while out walking on the Sussex Downs. Vanessa settled there in 1916, together with her children and the artist Duncan Grant, who was to share her life, and the latter's lover, David Garnett, who was later to marry Vanessa's own daughter, Angelica. Born in 1918, Angelica tells the story of life at Charleston in her autobiography *Deceived with Kindness* (London, Chatto & Windus/Hogarth Press, 1984). A child among this oddly "extended" family, she had time to observe the various husbands, wives, lovers, friends, and mistresses cohabiting in an atmosphere free of prejudice, though not always of jealousy.

Surrounded by an enclosed garden and embellished by what Angelica remembers as an "enormous" pond, from the outside the "large and compact" house looked like many others in the district. Inside, however, "stimulated by the interchange of visual ideas," Vanessa and Duncan furnished and painted the house in "subtle and glowing colors which splashed and streaked every surface, transforming walls, mantelpieces, doors, and furniture."

When energetic painters of the talent of Grant and Bell introduce fresco into a domestic atmosphere, one can be sure that their prime motivation was not mere economic necessity. Both had collaborated in the Omega Studios founded in 1913 by

On the mantelpiece at Charleston, a photo of Vanessa Bell taken around 1910.
The paneling, vases, and dishes were all painted "in-house" by Vanessa,
her children, or Duncan Grant.

The studio was shared by Vanessa Bell and Duncan Grant,
who together painted the walls, the mantelpiece,
the screen, the vases, and all the other objects.
They both admired Picasso who in turn took inspiration
from their work for his ceramics.

critic Roger Fry, in which the latter hoped to promote the abolition of the artificial distinction between "major" and "minor" arts, and encourage young artists to create their own furniture and objects. Duncan and Vanessa put these theories into practice in their country home, and, inspired by the examples of Matisse and Fauvism, joyously discovered how to transform the most unappealing and everyday objects into art.

Angelica admiringly describes her mother painting the bedroom walls in an audacious mix of "soot-black" and Venetian red, running up cotton chair covers, and shoring up shelves suffering under the weight of books. In the shared studio that Angelica was later to call the "citadel of the house," Grant and Bell were mutually electrified by each other's talent. At Charleston "the freedom she had discovered in her own life was expressed in painting," while her openness to the decorative arts encouraged visiting artists to treat the walls or the furniture in the same way as a canvas.

The true soul of the house, Vanessa ruled over the "quintessence of cultured society" of painters and writers at Charleston with an iron rod. By the end, the farmhouse, as Angelica herself concludes in her preface to Vanessa Bell's *Sketches in Pen and Ink* (Hogarth, 1997), "having accumulated the patina of twenty years of family life, was both familiar and necessary, known and trusted, both as a house and a refuge . . . A visual kingdom as well as a haven . . . it was not a possession. If the place was important, it was mainly as a setting for those who shared it."

FACING PAGE: Clive Bell's bedroom.
Vanessa painted the Louis XVI-style bed,
the rustic-looking table, and the walls.
Above: the bathroom. The wood panel
running round the tub was painted
by Richard Shone. All the doors have been
painted like pictures. Sitting on the Italian
chest of drawers, purchased in Rome,
a portrait of Vanessa's sister, Virginia Woolf;
also, canvases by Duncan Grant, among
which a "self-portrait with turban."

JEAN ODDES

Brut de brut

"Extravagant, *moi*? On the contrary, I think I'm extraordinarily reasonable. I put great store by things being adapted to their use and by the choice of correct materials: a chair should be for sitting on, a bathroom easy to hose down." Jean Oddes only grudgingly concedes that it is a slight surprise to see his motorcycle—a gleaming Guzzi—parked at the end of his bed. It's probably also a way of recapturing something of the genius of the place—after all, his loft standing at the rear of a courtyard was built from knocking through four old garages. As to his talent, it also results from the fusion of two different universes: studies in the history of art that resulted in a stint teaching on the other side of the Atlantic, and his training as a fresco painter at the center for the study of medieval civilization at Poitiers, in the shadow of the finest Romanesque cathedral in all France.

Jean Oddes might have taken the cloth, but contents himself instead with working to the sound of motets and masses under the watchful eye of a silver-gilt seventeenth-century bishop, a striking contrast with the monastically concrete walls and the wood floor washed down with bleach "for the way it softens the color."

This is the only visible sign of softness in what is a chillily masculine environment: a tile-topped table, two benches, a bedstead on casters, two wooden chairs—tree trunks barely touched by the carver's chisel—a bookcase with chicken-wire over the doors. But man too is fickle: Jean Oddes loathes and detests routine, the daily round, love in a cottage ("see you tonight, darling,"—how horrid!) and refuses to get hooked on things. Every now and again, he stages an "open-house day" when "Everything Must Go." And it all has to be begun again—preferably in a different way.

It was his taste for the ephemeral that saved his tears when the tarpaulin that had been covering the Madeleine church in Paris during its two-year overhaul had

In his residential loft—a former garage—Jean Oddes decided to keep the unfaced concrete walls;
all the openings for doors and windows are surprisingly narrow.
The armchair and metal-framed sofa were made to his own design.

Preceding pages: left, the wire over the bookcase; two seventeenth-century busts of bishops and Jean Oddes' motorcycle that he parks at the foot of his bed each night. The furniture is minimalist. At one end of the loft, the bed, with its metal bedstead on casters. On either side, telescopic wall lights. Jean Oddes in his chaise longue, a plywood replica of a Corbusier prototype. The bathroom is tiled black. Behind Jean Oddes' desk—as elsewhere in the whole loft—a built-in cupboard. Right: some pencil drawings.

to come down: the church painted on the canvas (and prettier than the real one) was by him. He displays the same gusto when organizing an event lasting a bare two hours—launching a perfume or showcasing a collection.

If he enjoys these explosive moments when he has to improvise, get his ideas across, and do so accurately and fast, very fast, Jean Oddes is in his element as an interior architect. Then, he has to understand people and urge them to express their own likes and dislikes without worrying about the strangulating dog-collar of interior design: good taste.

The only area where the professional tries to influence his clients, a representative cross-section of a recent social class, the Bobos (bourgeois bohemians), is lighting. After reading a few pages of Junichiro Tanizaki's *In Praise of Shadow* before bed, Oddes revels in mobilizing all the resources of lighting and obtaining just the right doses of shadow and illumination for each room, modulating and filtering almost scientifically. "But," the glistening biker opines before setting out to spend two hours pumping iron in an out-of-town sports center he revamped himself, "no one has invented anything more beautiful than a candle." In cupboards that run around the walls of the loft, concealing an office, a shower cubicle, a dressing-room, and a wealth of storage space, he stockpiles candles. All shapes and sizes—but all, without exception, white.

JANINE JANET

J

The Melancholy Museum

Though she's only recently left us, Janine Janet lives on in every single room of the apartment she inhabited for over fifty years with her husband, the painter Jean-Claude Janet. We are received in the Sleeping Beauty castle, where one can hear the muffled rumble of buses making their way to the Gare du Nord, by one of her enigmatic creatures: a limewood bust of a man studded with nails—he is, in fact, the Knave in a triptych, together with the King and Queen, designed for Balenciaga.

A museum in miniature, the drawing room contains countless specimens of her many-sided imagination: numerous watercolors, oils on canvas, ceramics, a God of the Forest, clad in birch bark, the Goddess of the Harvest, emerging from a golden wheat sheaf, a bust bristling with jade and madrepore, a gigantic stained-glass Harlequin, a burnished bronze stag, a tin and copper Tower of Babel, masks in patina leather. Chimeras, sphinxes, sirens, Silenuses, phoenixes—if Janine Janet's inspiration, infused as it was with ancient Greek culture, is rooted in mythology, the strangeness of her baroque interpretation masks consummate virtuosity.

In the beginning, she worked her magic in sculpture, a rough-and-tumble, masculine calling if ever there was one. Cocteau himself balked at the term "sculptor," preferring to dub "Madame" Janet, *une fée*. It was she who made the centaurs in *Le Testament d'Orphée* that still ride round and round in the memory of film-lovers everywhere. Cocteau was rocked on his heels: "More marvelous even than writing follies is to see them, in the flesh, before one."

Before going on to create "follies" for the Aga Khan's parties and for palaces in the Middle East, Janine Janet first set them up for any passer-by with eyes to see them. This was in the 1950s and 1960s, decades for which creative drive is only now beginning to be re-evaluated. Today, people walk past *haute couture* houses and don't give them

Born on Réunion Island, Janine Janet's childhood was spent surrounded by the corals
and shells that she was later to employ with such panache. The quartz and coral bust stands
at the entrance to the living room.

FACING PAGE: at the "feet" of the queen (who actually hasn't got any), a sculpture studded with nails, sits a man-sized, jointed wooden dummy from the nineteenth century. These pictures show some of Janine Janet's many sculptures: an Angel adorned with quartz and topaz, a Faun covered in birch bark, and the King, one of the nail busts designed for Balenciaga.

a second look: their windows look like magazines in which you can't tell the ads from the articles. As this hard-nosed approach is regularly doused with the unflappable wash of Japanese minimalism, we are a million miles away from the dazzling floor shows that great design houses once staged gratis every day in the capital's most chic storefronts.

Each had a house style—and a card-carrying window dresser to boot. Following a recommendation from the high priestess at Hermès, Annie Baumel, Janine Janet began working, uncredited, for Cristobal Balenciaga. Struck by her work, the Spanish master, though well-known for his severity, offered her carte blanche in what was a unique arrangement. Every year, in an agreement that was periodically renewed over two decades, the stipulation remained the same: Janet was to come up with the sculptural equivalent of his hugely elegant collections. Balenciaga did not even demand exclusive use of the services of this artist who understood him so well and whom he thought of almost as a sister. Dior, Givenchy, Nina Ricci, Cardin also called on her assistance, so she cast her magic spell up avenue Montaigne and down avenue George V, and people would stop dead in their tracks and gaze upon her creations.

Most of these short-lived wonders have long since been dispersed. You'd be lucky today to see the statues of the Four Elements designed for the *Queen Elizabeth II*, the crystal and gilded-silver ostensory intended for the Vatican, or the unicorns set up for the state visit of the Queen of the Belgians to London. But Janine Janet's talent was prolific, so her husband—the author of many portraits of his wife, as well as a much appreciated landscape painter in his own right—has been able to assemble an exhibition of her work to take place at the Musée de la Chasse in 2002. The museum also

serves as the Musée de la Nature, making it an ideal setting. Though her gifts were nurtured at the École des Beaux-Arts—where she modeled maquettes in wax, clay, and plaster before scaling them up according to the time-honored rules of her art— it was a girlhood spent on the island of Réunion that explains her attraction to all things marine, a fascination with the transformations of the mineral, vegetable, and animal worlds. At an age when children on Brittany's beaches turn out sandcastles, Janine was building palaces out of shells.

Janet the Circe often combines her chosen materials, shells and coral, wood and bronze, in complicated marquetry, making mirrors, bowls, and candelabras fit for a grotto decorated by some Italian prince in the seventeenth or eighteenth century. A far cry from today's eye-candy that melts into a mess of name-brand gewgaws. Nonetheless, giving a wide berth to products marketed so as to make cash tills ring out across five continents, one can occasionally glimpse hints of what is a necessarily more elitist striving for something unique, singular, understated.

Janine Janet's whole oeuvre is a response to such desires.

RIGHT: above the fireplace watched over by a bronze stag, the portrait of Janine Janet by her husband Jean–Claude Janet. ABOVE, plaster maquettes for other sculptures and, on the table, sketches, photos, exhibition memorabilia, and diverse magazine clippings.

The Leo Also Roars

*R*avage?" Devastate, pillage, lay waste: the dictionary entry is scary. This peaceable artistic duo, however, chose the signature simply because it is an amalgam of their two names: Clemens Rameckers and Arnold Van Geuns. They met thirty years ago at the Art School in Arnhem in central Holland and have been inseparable ever since, living and working together. Perhaps destiny has had a hand in it. Their zodiac sign is Leo. They were born the same year (1950), same month (August), well-nigh the same day (the 1st and the 8th) and they occupy the same place among their respective siblings (number three of five children).

In spite of promising beginnings in the gallery they opened in 1972 in the town of their birth, where they put on catwalk shows for young designers as well as launching their own collections, they quickly made up their minds to try their luck elsewhere, "gripped by a fear of getting stuck in a rut." Off they went to Paris where they met up with their compatriot, the stylist Li Edelkoort. They earned their keep as fashion stylists and business consultants. In tandem, of course.

Their geographical wanderings were aided and abetted by imaginary voyages. And so their travels continued. Imbued with history, great readers of biographies, regular visitors to the Louvre and the Musée Carnavalet, they drew and painted— in a style on friendly terms with the Antique and tinged with academicism—their very own gallery of heroes. Confident enough in their originality to acknowledge their influences: "We're not building on ruins but on memories, and we're ready to reinvent them."

Adam and Eve, Heloise and Abelard, Napoleon and Josephine, Louis XVI and Marie-Antoinette cover wallpapers, china, folding screens, smaller items of furniture

Painting directly on to the wood support as on to a medieval altarpiece, Clemens Rameckers and Arnold Van Geuns take inspiration from the crowned heads, saints' faces, and mythological heroes that make up their universe.

that are drawn in a good strong line, black on white or white on black, and enlivened with an invigorating dose of color.

The keynote is cheerfulness: "We don't create to take revenge, but to offer pardons." "The only thing that makes us really sad is having to sell. Either because it's been such a success—or else because there's still room for improvement."

Workaholics, they lock themselves away seven days a week in a studio near the place de la République lined with drawings from floor to ceiling. Hundreds more are piled up in cardboard boxes from which, by a process they've christened "cascade logic," emerge crockery, household linen, fabrics, and furniture.

And they begin by testing it all in their own, utterly "Ravaged," apartment.

"We are entirely self-sufficient," Arnold and Clemens declare in one voice. No time—no desire either—to join the Paris social whirl. "We are the Greta Garbos of interior design," they jokingly remark. Except that, known primarily in the business and among serious collectors, they cannot be said to be stars exactly. Regrets? None at all. "We derive our pleasure from doing the work, not from carving out a career."

Furniture, ceramics, household linen—Ravage's designs are all stamped
with their unmistakable hallmark. Fantastically colorful, fantastically elaborate,
they possess just the kind of lyrical, European style that Americans love.

MANOLO NÚÑEZ

Philosophy on the Move

*H*e first thought long and hard, hesitating between two equal passions: theater and architecture. In order to reconcile them—and rather than designing luxury villas for clients who hum and ha interminably about where to put the fireplace or the direction the kitchen should face—the Catalan, Manolo Núñez, chose instead to construct ministries, faculty buildings, official residences, and, needless to say, theaters. All places that require "staging," all spaces that call for a grand design. Not for him though delusions of grandeur: outraged by the cost of recent white elephants (Paris has more than its fair share), Núñez makes a point of adhering to deadlines and hard-nosed budgets, be they in dollars, pounds, yens, escudos, or francs—or, daresay, in the future euro.

One exception to such belt-tightening policies: the spectacular fortress he has built himself in the Ampurdan countryside half an hour from the French frontier. He took his inspiration from the so-called Indian houses that Catalans back from the Americas in the nineteenth century commissioned from local artisans. Closer to his own personal universe and lying just opposite in the hills is the Château de Pubol that formerly belonged to his old friend Salvador Dalí and where Dali's wife Gala spent the last years of her life.

With its sober, almost minimalist, furnishings, his Villa Redonna can certainly not be regarded as "Dalírious." The open doors leading to empty corridors, the geometric arcades framing the sky, the monumental staircases make one think of another painter entirely: De Chirico, whose Disquieting Muses will doubtless attend many a future production in the amphitheater that Manolo Núñez has also designed for them.

After collaborating in the early days with Ricardo Boffil under the auspices of the famous "Taller," Manolo Núñez has written plays, acted as artistic director, painted stage-sets, and even strode the boards himself, to the point that he can

The curved sweeps of the swimming pool are flanked
by a pair of staircases that meet at the doorstep.

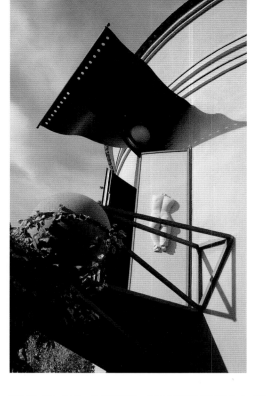

The patio is planted with orange and lemon trees. LEFT: the stone table

on which meals can be taken in peace, sheltered from the tramontana.

ABOVE: the painted sheet-steel awning above the front door.

The seventeen-foot triangular diving-board.

choose today between being Dom Juan and designing the Statue of the Commander, but the great race is the one against time. He already has an office in Paris, another in Barcelona, and projects on the go more or less everywhere.

He has to make do with spending a few weeks a year at most in his villa in Spain with his wife and children. Even in highest summer, it is never too hot: the walls are thick and the windows narrow. All the windows in the living room and the bedroom give onto a closed-in patio planted with orange and lemon trees sheltered from the tramontana wind. To refresh the eyes and the body, there is always the turquoise swimming pool. In spite of its impressive dimensions, it could never be ratified for the Olympics: the architect provocateur, who claims to loathe architecture, has designed it in the shape of a bow, like an amphitheater. In fact, what he actually hates is architecture that is content to propose technical and functional solutions to every imaginary "problem" it encounters. For Manolo Núñez, a house provides a stage on which life can be played out: his mission, his ambition, is to make the life within freer, more open, indeed more exquisite.

LEFT: the bedrooms open onto a circular corridor. Like the bathroom, the bedrooms possess triangular windows. ABOVE: the library with shelving running round the iron stairway.

The long dining room table is made of
polished red concrete.
On the wall, a geometric arrangement of
plates that reminds one of a Welsh dresser.
Like the lazy Susan, but unlike the classic
cane chairs, it was built by local craftsman.

Sculpture Fit to Live In

*M*inas likes silver. Not the silver coins you earn, spend, gamble with, or squirrel away. The sort he makes jewelry out of, shiny like pebbles, or which he transforms into the finest tableware, whose pure lines and sensual curves evoke Cycladic art, a five-thousand year-old civilization that Minas, though an Athenian, celebrates and continues in sculptures that fill his house.

Choosing a site for the house was simplicity itself: Mykonos. Not the sea, sun, and sex paradise that outstrips Saint-Tropez, but the real Cycladic isle, with its untouched beaches hewn from the granite. Minas' materials? The same as those used by the earliest inhabitants of the island: earth, stone, wood. As to color, the question did not even arise—white, in and out. Completely at one with the landscape, the house comprises a succession of smooth-angled cubes that make it look as though it has been standing there for centuries. A second glance though dispels this impression; the throw of the stairs, the shape of the doors and windows through which pours a cloudless blue sky go well beyond traditional models and display the Minas touch.

Many of his pieces are in silver, but Minas also works in gold, steel, marble, and porcelain. Unique pieces, all signed, fresh from his Athens studio, or else in limited editions made by the silversmith, Georg Jensen. Be it a necklace or a goblet, a watch or a corkscrew, Minas always strives to wed effective design to visual pleasure. And to fill one with the urge to stroke their swelling surfaces inspired by plant or mineral forms. For Minas, nature, that he has been studying since he was fifteen, is an inexhaustible reservoir of beauty. And it is in his white-painted house, far from the madding crowd, that he can best feel its nearness.

Minas' whitewashed house hovers between the blue of the sky above and that of the sea below.
Standing amidst the gray stone, the house, like some elongated sculpture,
resembles the jewelry and other objects for which he has become famous.

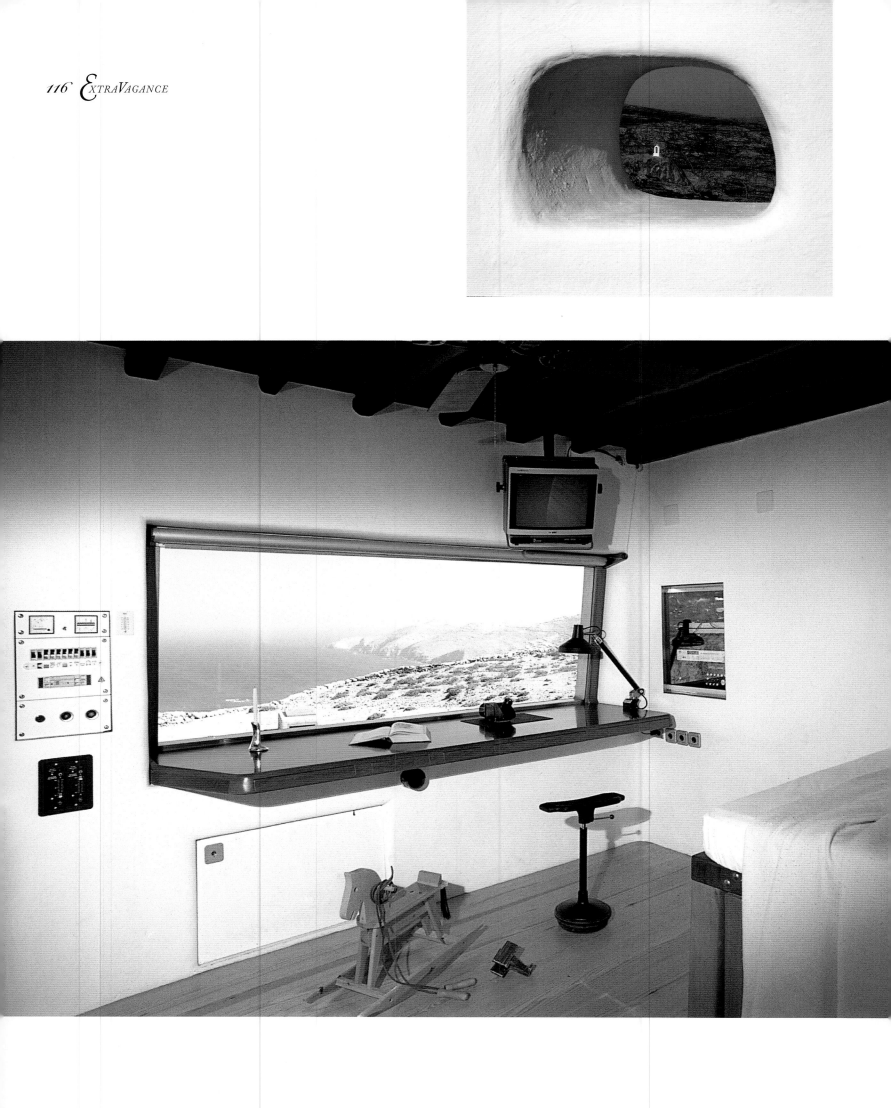

Perfectly at one with the landscape,
and far removed from the overcrowded beaches
and throbbing nightlife of Mykonos,
the house that Minas built provides
the designer with ample opportunity to get
back to his roots. There he can take a quiet
vacation with his family and spend his days
studying and working in landscapes
that offer him so much inspiration.

Marrying Their Talents

*W*hen you hear that someone "lives like an artist," images of an unbuttoned Bohemia come to mind—going to bed at all hours, quaffing cocktails, shooting the breeze in cafés, working in the white-heat of enthusiasm, mood-swinging from passion to depression and from break-up to breakdown—well, no, actually, the Garoustes will never star in a film of that particular genre.

In 1984, Gérard and Elizabeth ensconced their then young sons in a fine seventeenth-century town house on the edge of a wood at Marcilly-sur-Eure. "And," as Elizabeth has said, "we did everything ourselves."

Everything, meaning? The sculpture, paintings, and frescos are signed Gérard Garouste no less, a talent whom Maurice Rheims, a man well qualified to judge such matters, has dubbed the finest French painter today. Though he also works in every room, he has fitted out two studios. The first is set aside for sculpture, while the second, built up against the hill, is the size of a cathedral, big enough for his enormous canvases.

As for the furniture, fabrics, lamps, and other objects, some have been there since the beginning, while others are just passing through before being carted off to a client or a gallery—all creations of the Garouste-Bonetti duo.

Elizabeth and Mattia first met in the late 1970s at the Privilège, Fabrice Emer's erstwhile mythical club, not to dance, but to decorate the restaurant. This encounter marked the start of their professional association. Presented in 1981, their first collection proved a sensation—and a scandal. Invited by Jeanne Gambert de Loche, director at Jansen, they scattered hammer-worked iron wardrobes, papier-maché console-tables, and calf-upholstered chairs around the white and gold salons on the rue Royale.

Thus, without even seeking it, Elizabeth Garouste and Mattia Bonetti achieved overnight fame. Not for Andy Warhol's easy quarter of an hour, but for a quarter of a century plus. And it's far from over yet.

Standing beneath a canvas by Gérard Garouste, a white and gray
earthenware cabinet on wrought–iron feet, signed Garouste–Bonetti.

*In the living room, chauffeuses and sofa upholstered
in Lelièvre damask between a pair of Coromandel folding
screens. The furniture forms part of the Topkapi Collection.
Flanking the fireplace Gérard Garouste's "Indiennes."
ABOVE, a console whose papier-maché caryatids were inspired
by the "Venus" of Willendorf.*

Every inch of the house is imbued with art.
FACING PAGE: in the stairway, Gérard
Garouste's graffiti on the yellow paintwork.
Beneath a dark-wood corner-table, a plaster cast.
ABOVE LEFT: a painted-wood chest, adorned
with irregularly shaped pieces of steel on which
stands a mask that doubles as a lamp. Made
by Garouste-Bonetti for En Attendant Les
Barbares.
ABOVE RIGHT: Gérard's own black hat, stand-
ing, like a sculpture, on the period console.

Stuffed with historical references, the florid baroque of these "two barbarians" feeds the empty feeling left by modernist belt-tightening. Their prolific creativity has gone like a dose of salts through a host of designers (and provided mountains of work for a gaggle of copycats). Their insolence and grandeur have whetted the appetites of super-rich customers who'd thought they'd seen it all—to an extent unparalleled since the heydays of Carlos de Bestegui and Marie-Laure de Noailles. Not many Frenchmen though among the billionaires who meet up with them at the Ritz or the Crillon—unless they are cultured collectors of the type who go in for Jean-Michel Frank or Emilio Terry.

The lawyer Mr. Woo, for example, is hardly a next-door neighbor: he hails from Hong Kong. Giving Elizabeth and Mattia carte blanche to realize a dream he just could not get to gel, the house has four storeys and the project was ongoing for four years. Every element has been designed and made to measure. Flown in from Paris, the painters stayed on for five months, gilding the walls.

Then there was the even more extravagant Japanese gentleman, mad about tigers (and perhaps mad *tout court*), for whom the team thought up numberless pieces of furniture, objects, fabrics (some costing $1,000 a yard) adorned with tigers, every-thing being carved, chased, embroidered in France.

Their encounters with the fashion world have been no less spectacular. They were behind Christian Lacroix's fuschia and orange showrooms, as well as the pastel-colored plastic packaging for Nina Ricci's perfume and cosmetic range,

Gérard Garouste has the run of two sizable studios on his private estate but can take to drawing anywhere and everywhere in the house, often composing preparatory gouache sketches in the library sitting on a wooden chair. Posing with Elizabeth in front of the earthenware cabinet she designed for Néotu in 1981.
FAR RIGHT: the branchiform display-rack Elizabeth made herself for hanging necklaces and bracelets.

a notable example of the cross-pollination between elitist extravaganza and consumer marketing. Another hit: the carafe, glass, and ashtray for Ricard, a favorite café triplet that all too often "falls" into the bags of light-fingered barflies. And they're wise flies: the threesome has long since become a "must-have."

Art galleries have not been sluggards either: Néotu in Paris, and David Gill in London, to mention but two, are committed fans of the tandem that work their magic out of a huge joint studio in Belleville. Thursday night, Elizabeth takes off in her car and goes back to the countryside, her family, and her animals: cows and calves, pigs and brooding hens.

Some artists, such as Picasso and Warhol, transformed their homes into museums while they were still alive, filling rooms to the brim with art treasures as if they were bank vaults, then leaving it all to fractious heirs to squabble over with an accompanying thunder of writs and sworn testimonies. Not the Garoustes. Their house lives and breathes talent, hard work, and imagination, but there is no hint of ostentatious wealth or investment planning. "True luxury," Elizabeth reminds us with a sigh, "is time." She too would like to get her hands on some, to travel, read, or tend the garden a bit more. Time, of course, but what else? Nothing money can buy: "For me to possess something is to close the loop and that's something like death. I like to keep my distance, so my wants are never satisfied. It's what's called desire."

What could the Garoustes ever want for? Now renowned artists, they enjoy the life of quiet opulence that they have chosen in a house that resembles them and that even conceals, like the fairy-tale castle, mysterious attic rooms that have never been explored. Elizabeth has never had a mind to do so. "A Mannerist ethnologist," rather than a painstaking historian, she prefers to find sustenance in a dreamworld Middle Ages, in an enchanted Africa, a recreated Venice. Rather than open old trunks, she has chosen to simply close her eyes and, gently rocked by the Angel of the Bizarre, to dream.

Distressed Chic

*W*hen Liza first met Nicholas at Holland Park School, London, she was fourteen. It was love at first sight. In spite of her protests, she was packed off to a convent in Mexico City to continue her studies.

Nicholas followed, however, and the romance blossomed. And, as we're no longer among Verona's Montagues and Capulets but in 1970s London, both sets of parents eventually softened. And it was a good thing too: Liza Bruce and Nicolas Alvis Vega grew up, flourished, and became successful together, initially in New York, before returning to London. She in fashion, dressing battalions of celebs out of her shop on Pont Street (Kate Moss, Naomi Campbell, Jennifer Lopez, etc., etc.), he in the art world, organizing exhibitions, following a parallel career as a designer all the while.

So their life has been one long fairy tale. And the house? Well, it depends what you mean. Chipped paint, torn wallpaper, furniture on its last legs—over time they'd lovingly arranged it into something that might give those who can relax only in clean lines and polished surfaces a bit of a turn. Tastes beg to differ, however, and there are arguments on both sides. Feelings, too.

A certain down-at-heel gentility that rejects all things new and shiny has always enjoyed a good pedigree in Britain. The tradition is today seconded by a vogue for the antique that has made many a deluxe secondhand-clothes dealer rich and explains the hunt for vintage Levis in jeans shops.

"Shabby chic," as it is known, is a less purist affair, since it is not confined to particular makes or periods, and allows for bold strokes of mixing and matching. The trend corresponded to a period of belt-tightening, in which prices had to be cut to the quick.

Meals are taken on a cast–iron table painted white; the gilded wooden armchairs
have definitely been in the wars, while the fireplace
was cobbled together out of recovered masonry. Furniture by Alvis Vega.

It was not a question of playing at poverty, more of cutting one's flat to suit one's purse, and of making good and patching up wherever they could.

For their part, Liza and Nicolas went further: they made their Victorian dwelling in Shepherd's Bush look something like a squat. This was in reaction, Liza says, to the huge shapeless loft in which they'd lived for a time.

The "anti-loft" was divided into any number of minuscule rooms. It was anti-design too, since the rooms were filled with oddments of old furniture: Louis XV sofa, nineteenth-century bathtub (see pages 2 and 3). Anti-rich, since it was cobbled together out of materials that had all seen better days. But the veneer of nonchalance, the wholly original approach to comfort, and the seemingly untoward juxtapositions, all concealed a conscious striving for scenic effect. Each room was treated like a picture which, as Nicolas put it, required far more effort than a conventional revamp.

Later occupiers came along and did their own conversion: the house was eventually sold and renovated. As for Liza and Nicolas, today they live in an elegant Kensington apartment.

PRECEDING PAGES: the dining room.
A pleasant mix of period furniture (such as the
eighteenth-century banquette) and of designer
"making-do."
LEFT: the poetic yet Spartan bathroom, with
a giant shell in guise of a basin.
ABOVE: the bedroom under the eaves comprises
an iron-frame bed, a pair of wooden tables,
and a shelf above the fireplace that does for
a bookshelf.

Beneath the portrait of Liza Bruce and Alvis Vega,
a view of a kitchen that seems to have little patience with modern
creature comforts. RIGHT: the floorboards were stripped but the peeling
walls were left as they were. The violet emulsion painted
on the windows produces an eerie light.

Paradise Lost. A Walk on the Barbès Side.

Three years ago, Roland Beaufre was living on rue de Paradis. The street is dedicated to cut-crystal in all its forms and each storefront drowned in glassware vies to outshine its neighbor. Though the business itself mobilizes hundreds of TV ads and millions in stock, there have been no noticeable effects on an area that remains dull as dishwater. In 1990, the street even lost its advertising museum that upped sticks to join its mentor, the Musée des Arts Décoratifs, within the Louvre complex. So Roland too flew the nest, convinced that Paradise could no longer be found in Paris. Homesick for Tangiers, he searched high and low for somewhere that would alleviate the want of color, warmth, and scent. He found it in Barbès, in front of the Tati department store, whose pink plastic bags fill the quarter (and beyond) with color. Hard by Montmartre and not far from Pigalle, the boulevard Barbès, unlike its noisier neighbors, doesn't attract much in the way of tourism or thuggery. As soon as the stores shut up shop, the little enclave is pretty quiet, with regulars sitting in African, Arab, and Indian restaurants as well as old residential buildings, their entryways polished to a shine. Roland's own building combines a pink marble foyer with 1900s style stained glass in the stairwell.

When he first discovered his three-room apartment that gives onto the courtyard, it was in much the same ilk. Desperately classical. Worse than just ugly—boring. But Roland, attracted by the ethnic mix of the markets, and the Far Eastern delis and the shelves weighed down with bubus, heard the cry of the muezzin from the local mosque and made up his mind to stay. He's enjoying it too.

Having a *pied-à-terre* in Paris that he has injected with color, decorated with imagination, and furnished with a light touch, allows him to fly off to Tangiers and to the family house and garden planted with cypress trees, jasmine, and laurel,

In the bedroom, Roland has hung a cowhide above the bed covered with a blanket found at a Barbès outdoor market. Lamp by Thierry Peltraut. Moroccan carpet.

In a corner of the orange room, a chair in patinated metal with bicycle handlebars serving as a back. FACING PAGE: the one-of-a-kind table is the result of a collaboration between Dixon and Dubreuil. It is of patinated bronze with copper soldering. On the wall hangs a 1960s carpet with a psychedelic pattern.

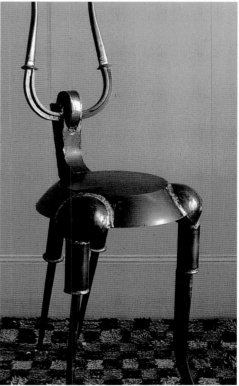

at the drop of a hat. He spends all his vacations there, and at least one whole week a month. An eminently reasonable lifestyle: there is no end to the list of travelers who originally went for a day or two but who never managed to leave the place. For Truman Capote, Tennessee Williams, William Burroughs, Allen Ginsberg, and Jean Genet, Tangiers served as a fixed point in their passionate, often turbulent lives. Delacroix brought back thousands of sketches from his trips there and Henri Matisse discovered light. Author Paul Bowles meanwhile found "wisdom and ecstasy."

Roland Beaufre regularly comes back from Tangiers laden with spices, bunches of flowers, and of course a nostalgia for sun and sea. His designer interior contains the odd vase and carpet, but he has never succumbed to the temptations of folklore.

Prior to becoming a photographer who loves taking pictures of domestic spaces and a contributor to numerous magazines, Roland Beaufre (who shot the material for the present publication) initially studied architecture at the École des Beaux-Arts before launching the organization "En Attendant les Barbares" with Frédéric de Luca in 1984. The idea was to have furniture and objects created by young designers made by top-flight craftsmen in Morocco: first up, Garouste and Bonetti, soon followed by Jean-Philippe Gleizes. After a couple of years, however, Roland's time was being devoured by manufacture and distribution problems, and

he threw it up. He kept the friends he had made though, and continues to monitor their progress.

His house contains early pieces by Tom Dixon, André Dubreuil, and Patrick Nagar, all of whom he knew and gave support to in the early days. He has not been afraid to juxtapose collection pieces with a cowhide, a carpet stumbled on in a souk, or a garishly patterned microfiber blanket.

Red stripes banded in black bravely mount to the living-room ceiling, while eternal summer reigns in a bedroom painted with a sun motif. The bathroom is a Rhapsody in Blue, where designs fresh from a Hockney swimming pool float about on the tiling. Studiously white, the office does what it's told: though some of the publications that line the walls are dedicated to dynamiting art, fashion, and interior design, when it comes to his own house, Roland Beaufre has elected a less explosive, if still dynamic, approach.

The stripes were hand-painted in one day. The sofa and stool with jersey

slipcovers date from the 1970s. Red sheet metal sculpture by Ciborovski.

FAR LEFT: "Spine" chair by Dubreuil and a table by Tom Dixon.

Stagecraft

*W*hen Daniel Hourdé is at work in his loft, he leaves the door open. To get to it though, you have first to find the little street a hundred yards or so from the Seine, be told the code to open the entry way, go down a long corridor, and cross a courtyard. Not many unwelcome visitors here then. But at least invited guests shouldn't think he's not in, and slink off disappointed: Daniel Hourdé works with the music on, and even if you're expected, he just doesn't hear you coming.

So, you in go without knocking and bump into a naked ephebe, who, fleeing, pulls on his jeans and T-shirt, and asks: "I come back tomorrow?" It's the model. "Yes, we'll carry on tomorrow," Daniel Hourdé replies. He's the sculptor.

The glass-roofed studio is in the middle. On either side (there are no partitions), there lie the master bedroom and a room for his fifteen-year-old son who used to board out in the provinces but who's come back to Paris to get into a "good school," one of those that open the door to the French administrative or business schools. But his dad is worried: "He doesn't seem to know what he wants to do." When he was fifteen, Daniel Hourdé certainly knew what he *didn't* want to do: law, literature, science, medicine. He'd already purchased a few articles of African tribal art with his pocket money. A shrewd business head, he had soon opened a gallery of ethnic art in Saint-Germain-des-Prés (in association with Philippe Ratton, a boyhood friend) though he carried on a career in the visual arts he had begun after a stint at the Beaux-Arts in 1975. His work went against the grain, ignoring fashion, novel techniques, and attention-seeking alike. His disturbingly realist charcoal drawings and bronzes are more akin to Rodin or Bourdelle than to his contemporaries. Strong men, muscular and sinewy, walking, in motion. How tall? Lifesize. And "size" is the operative word. Like their maker, all stand over six foot tall.

The velvet-covered gilded chairs and sofa,

part of a nineteenth-century Neapolitan suite,

stand in a bedroom that is separated from the studio by glass.

"I carry these sizes in my hands. I just couldn't make anything else," he comments. Daniel Hourdé refuses to say much else about his work, however. Simply, "If I was not in this business, I'd go mad."

He might be taken for a theater director, though. In the studio, it's just like being on stage. In the evening, the lighting strengthens and dramatizes the contrast between the dark walls, the sumptuous velvets, the dramatic paintings, the raw steel, the patinated gold. Except for the bed raised up on a dais, one searches in vain for somewhere comfortable to perch. The sofa and chairs, a nineteenth-century suite from Naples, were chosen more for their quality carpentry than for sitting on. While Daniel Hourdé waits for the entire floor to be relaid in black granite, there are a few Eastern carpets upon which to lounge. Several fine pieces stand dotted about the place. They haven't found a permanent resting-place as yet: an Italian marquetry table, a plump Dutch sideboard. What is unlikely ever to be moved are the improvised bookshelves made out of building materials and beams which, quite literally, weigh a ton or two.

Hundreds of volumes line the shelves, showing a healthy intellectual appetite. The first few alphabetically arranged rows (Aragon, Artaud, Bataille, Baudrillard, Céline, Cioran) testify to a nourishing if eclectic diet of French high culture.

Further away, in both space and time: a Peruvian mummy; an Egyptian sarcophagus; a whole stash of African art. Then a superb forked branch, lying horizontally on a plinth, is most intriguing. Richard Deacon? Jean Degottex? "I picked it up during a walk in the woods," the master of the house informs us. It's all a question of eye. And of taking the time to go on walks. Without rushing. Daniel Hourdé openly confesses to being "unhurried, a *flaneur*, nonchalant, verging on the lazy." "Cool," perhaps as they say in advertising agencies that launch let-it-all-hang-out styles and perfumes that smell of zilch.

Cool, but sporty. Supple as an eel, like Romeo, our sculptor scampers up the rope ladder that hangs from the bedroom ceiling. It goes up through a trapdoor in the mirrored glass and leads to the floor above—where lives his Juliet.

Facing page: the bookcase Daniel Hourdé made from a few iron beams and other building materials. Above: in the bedroom: the bed erected on a black marble dais. The wardrobes are closed off with velvet drapes instead of doors.
The sculptor's favorite colors, red and midnight blue, can even be found in the kitchen, where he has "encased" the fridge.

Scandinavian Baroque: a Castle in Denmark

In 1648, King Christian IV of Denmark, who had already lost one eye on the field of battle, closed the other forever. He thus never had the chance of meeting Louis XIV, who had ascended his throne in 1643, aged five. It's a pity they missed each other. If he'd lived longer and visited Versailles, not only could Christian have chatted with Louis about their respective subjects, concerning whom, like all those in senior positions, they probably had much to complain, but he could have broached another, even more scintillating, subject: the architecture of their respective residences in which they invested so much energy and money. Like the Sun King, if on a more modest scale, Christian IV too was an ambitious builder. His passion for hard drinking and for all life's pleasures has somewhat overshadowed this vocation, but posterity has seen him right: Denmark owes most of her churches and palaces to this monarch and, for this reason, Christian has become a national hero.

All self-respecting kings build palaces to publicize their power and to keep the populace happy by proxy. Christian IV, however, derived additional pleasure from his building activities. Fascinated by technology, his residences are three-dimensional experiments based on the inventions he noted in his personal papers. For example, he perfected a mechanism that allowed the royal hand to raise and lower the drawbridge from within. He also had pipes concealed in the walls through which music played by an invisible orchestra could be piped to other rooms in the palace. As can be imagined, visitors at the time could hardly believe their ears.

This Heath Robinsonesque side was shared by his daughter-in-law, Sophie Amalie, wife of Frederik III, who had a "chair lift" constructed connecting two floors in her apartments. One day, the operator in charge of this ancestor of the present-day elevator lost control of the rope and, in trying to prevent the whole contraption crashing to the ground, crushed his hand to a pulp.

An elaborate ivory cup on a table in the Marble Room that
Frederik III had redecorated around 1670.

Early in the seventeenth century, the royal palace had been little better than an antiquated castle thirty miles out of Copenhagen. Neither site nor residence were particularly conducive to a young monarch like Christian. He bought up vast tracts of land to the east of the city and had them transformed into parkland, then constructing a pleasure pavilion before turning his attention to the principal task. The new chateau, twice the size of the old, was erected between 1613 and 1615. Completed in 1624, it was named Rosenborg, the "Castle of Roses," in homage to Queen Kirsten Munk whose coat-of-arms bears three roses. Utterly representative of Danish architecture of the time, it was a three-storey brick construction embellished in sandstone. A sizeable tower to one side, three smaller ones to the other, and above all, an impressive moat, trumpeted the fact that this was no minor manor. Adorned and enriched by four royal generations that resided there in the seventeenth and eighteenth centuries, Rosenborg remained the royal residence until the nineteenth. Today, it has become a public museum, though it remains marked by its first occupant, Christian IV. The Winter Room, the Long Hall (an audience chamber), and the Writing Closet, moreover, remain intact. The Winter Room, with its ninety-six pictures set into oak paneling, offers unique examples of Flemish painting. The ceiling, showing a battle between the Giants and the Gods painted by Pieter Issacsz. around 1620, was raised in 1705.

There are other paintings in the Writing Closet, including scenes from *Orlando Furioso* on the ceiling, probably by Francis Cleyn, who was subsequently to work for Christian's sister, Anne, who, on marrying James I, became Queen of England.

Refurbished by Frederik III around 1670 in an overblown baroque style, the floor of the Marble Room is original in a checkerboard pattern of various sizes and colors. The scagliola walls and the stucco ceiling with its exuberant sculptures were executed by an Italian, Francesco Bruno.

Queen Sophie Amalie had the bedroom where Christian IV died redecorated in the "Chinese" style that became voguish in the 1660s. Wainscoting and doors are

Christian IV's bedroom that Queen Sophie Amalie had refurbished in the
"Chinese" style that became voguish around 1660.
FOLLOWING PAGES: Christian VI's apartments. Dutch tapestries made around 1685 depicting
scenes from the life of Alexander the Great. The banquette and stools are Venetian.
The corner cupboards contain silver and vermeil grooming essentials.

*FACING PAGE: the mother-of-pearl
and ivory inlaid guitar bears the initials of
Frederik's IV's sister, Sophie Hedevig.
ABOVE: the birdcage built around 1770
that was supposedly the inspiration behind
Hans Christian Andersen's "Nightingale."
ABOVE RIGHT: Frederik IV's hall in which
the walls were hung with Gobelins tapestries.*

painted *façon écaille* (i.e. imitation tortoiseshell), and they are inset with small panels showing landscapes, ships, and interiors in gold filigree against a green lacquer ground.

In the same vein, but more precious still, the Lacquered Chamber is ornamented with other chinoiseries inlaid with turquoise and mother-of-pearl. The unusually dark interior sought perhaps to suggest that the room was to serve as a jewel case for its most precious gem, the Queen herself.

At the beginning of the eighteenth century and before building a new Summer Palace, Frederik IV commissioned two spectacular projects: the Mirror Cabinet and the Glass Cabinet. The former is a pocket-size version of the Hall of Mirrors in Versailles. Both walls and ceiling are entirely clad in mirror-glass, as is the center of the parquet floor, perhaps to serve a baroque equivalent of "What the Butler Saw;" this is not as unlikely as it sounds since Frederik housed a collection of erotica in an adjoining room. The Glass Cabinet was created for his own collections; no less than one thousand pieces, several hundred being given to him in 1709 during a visit to Venice.

The château had become too small. Frederik IV went on to build others and Rosenberg gradually became what it is today: a museum for ceremonial weapons and silverware, the Crown Jewels and other sorts of valuable objects.

Rosenborg served as the royal residence on two further occasions. In 1794, after the great fire of Christianborg, and again in 1801, during the English siege of Copenhagen, when Nelson annoyingly kept the Danish monarch awake night after night.

A Taxi Named Desire

For transportation of an amorous nature, ring Tobias. His taxis, you can be sure, will take you to the doors of Nirvana.

Like so many people thirty years ago, in the age of Peace and Love, Tobias set off for India and discovered Goa. He came back a hippie and so he has remained ever since. Every year he goes off on his travels, the three month breather he needs to be able to face London town with its gray skies, rain, and noise.

Dressed, whatever the weather, in tunic or caftan, draped in a silk stole, Tobias looks at the world through rose-tinted spectacles. Literally. His optimism and imagination beguiled men like Tom Conran, the owner of the famous Notting Hill delicatessen, and Momo, a former associate of Smaïn in Paris, whose tajines and couscous attract London VIPs like a magnet.

This fashion-conscious twosome joined in financial partnership with Tobias who could thus make his dream come true: a cab company, Karma Kab, whose three cars have found a ready clientele, happy to take a trip to India for the price of a short taxi ride.

Photographers, rock musicians, advertising, and fashion folk all vie to reserve his fleet of Austin Ambassadors. This venerable model, ideal for India's potholed streets, is unlikely to escape in a car chase, but Tobias's customers are not trying to break the land-speed record and listen attentively when their driver quotes the Zen teaching: "To travel is more important than to arrive."

To do your traveling—by the trip, by the hour, or even by the day—you have the choice between "Honeymoon," with white flowers and interior, "Safari," upholstered in "panther" velvet, and "Flower Power," whose mauve-and-fuschia livery would have earned the plaudits of the late Barbara Cartland. Evocative of the

One of Karma Kab's three taxis,

interior by the mosaic artist Pierre Mesguich, whose design,

at Tobias's request, derives from the palaces of Rajahstan.

Amber Palace, the jewel of Rajahstan, it was designed by Pierre Mesguich. A mix of mosaic, mirrors, and Japanese pebbles, mounted on transparent tulle worthy of a *haute couture* frock. This begs the question as to why a designer rushed off his feet in Paris, London, and Barcelona studios, and constantly in demand for massive frescoes or princely swimming pools, should have bothered himself with Tobias's kitsch imaginings. "For the fun of it, and out of friendship," he replies. Maybe also for the example it gives. Though a retired hippie, Tobias has done well out of his Karma, and his project represents a clever bit of "re-engineering." His fame, and his customer base, has now even crossed the Channel. A few times a year, at the collection launches, he accompanies his favorite top-flight models about Paris on their arduous wanderings, from the Ritz to the Carrousel du Louvre, from the Plazza to the Trocadéro. With some restful religious music in the background, incense (sandalwood, patchouli), and soft, yielding cushions, Tobias, seconded by plastic divinities in glass containers, knows just what to do about those aching feet. And about that empty feeling in the soul.

Several times a year, come the Haute Couture *and* Prêt à Porter *collections,*
Tobias takes off for Paris.
Photographers and models alike adore his Flower Taxi.

*A*LBERTO
*P*INTO

Invitation to the Party

A man of excess! For Alberto Pinto, nothing can ever be too pretty, the house never too grand, the furnishings never too opulent . . . and the clients never too wealthy. Pet interior designer to the jet set—as well as Arab princes, multinational businessmen, and heads of state—Pinto set up his practice with fifty or so collaborators in a seventeenth-century *hôtel particulier* on the rue d'Aboukir, a stone's throw from the place des Victoires. He scarcely sees it today, however, since he's always flying about between Marrakech and New York, London and Montevideo, Riyadh and Madrid on gigantic projects, and so has little time to enjoy his sumptuous abodes. One of the last great parties of the millennium was thrown in his flat on the quai d'Orsay—long the home of Roger Vivier—shortly before all its glories went under the hammer at Sotheby's Inc.

Alberto Pinto's watchword is, "Everything palls—except change." Fifteen years ago he moved out of Paul Morand's large residence that stands at the foot of the Eiffel Tower. Today, however, it is not addresses he's into changing, but interiors: the nineteenth-century design that reigned supreme in this 800 m^2 habitation, in a building dating from the 1930s, might well be ousted by Art Deco. It was a very "Pintoesque" nineteenth century, of course, at once grandiose and eclectic—Russian, Italian, English furniture rubbing shoulders with German baroque and Napoleon III, all surrounded by a farrago of bronze, silver, rock-crystal *objets*, china, and Bohemian glasswork.

Pinto's trademark as an interior artist is a taste for color and combination, for profusion and exuberance, but these are also expressive of his true personality. Though he studied at the Louvre art school, went through the Beaux-Arts in Paris, and set up shop in New York, he was, and is, a man of the Mediterranean who

For the large salon, Alberto Pinto recreated an eclectic atmosphere typical of an early nineteenth-century Russian interior: the table is Austrian, the ten gouaches in the style of Pompeii hark back to the days of the "Grand Tour," while the chandelier is Russian.

looks back nostalgically on a boyhood spent in Morocco. "I grab ideas at the souk or in Indian or Mexican markets, instead of in books and museums like the majority of my colleagues," he remarks.

Who knows though whether the apartments he fitted out in the Élysée Palace are ever bathed in sunlight. Alberto Pinto confides only that the Chiracs—like Yves Saint Laurent, Jean-Luc Lagardère, and Lauren Bacall—are old friends. It must be admitted that Alberto Pinto has lots of friends, but he's amply equipped to receive them, doing so in the utmost luxury. His twelve historic dinner services (Compagnie des Indes, Sèvres, Gien, Creil, Tiffany, etc.) stretch to sixty covers, while the vermeil ceremonial plate engraved with the Orloff coat-of-arms, the innumerable pieces of silverware, and the Murano and Baccarat glass allow for infinite variation in table setting.

With Pinto, boredom comes from sameness. He escapes only rarely on vacation, to his inevitably superb house on Corsica, finding it more to his taste to spend time decorating an Argentine estancia or a Fifth Avenue triplex, or designing a yacht (one of his specialties) or a private jet: to date, he has delivered no less than seven—some of which measure 43,000 square feet (4000 m²)—with the same attention as his other projects.

All are equipped right down to the teaspoons and the paintings on the walls. Ready for occupation.

The furniture in the emerald-velvet-draped dining room is Russian, though here the chandelier is of Irish origin.
A superb collection of Chinese porcelain runs round the walls.

Acknowledgments

The authors and editors wish to express their sincere thanks to all the owners and decorators whose homes and work are featured in this book.

Special thanks also go to everyone who helped Roland Beaufre during the photo shoots: Alexandra d'Arnoux (André Dubreuil), Jean-Pascal Billaud (Marco de Gueltz, Minas), Marie-France Boyer (Mark Brazier-Jones, Tom Dixon, Janine Janet, Paul Jones), Dominique Dupuich (Vanessa Bell, Fornasetti, the Lalannes, Jean Oddes, Pierre et Gilles, Ravages), César Garçon (Deyan Sudjic), François Jonquet (Gilbert & George), Lisa Lovatt-Smith (Andrew Logan, Manolo Núñez, Pierre et Gilles, Denis Severs).

Roland Beaufre particularly thanks his agency, Top, who have represented his work for over twenty years. Special thanks also to Christiane Germain and Alexandra d'Arnoux.

The editor thanks Quentin Deslandes and Albine Harent for their assistance with the book.

Further Reading

On Fornasetti, Patrick Mauriès and Ettore Sottsass's *Fornasetti* (London: Thames and Hudson, 1998).
On Gilbert & George, the interview with David Sylvester in the catalog, *Rudimentary Pictures* (Los Angeles/London, 1999).
On Vanessa Bell, the book by her daughter, Angelica Garnett: *Deceived with Kindness* (London: Pimlico Paperbacks, 1995), and her granddaughter Virginia Nicholson: *A Bloomsbury House and Garden* (London: Frances Lincoln, 1997).

To Visit

Pierre Loti (pages 10 to 17): Maison Pierre Loti, 141 rue Pierre-Loti, 17300 Rochefor, France.
Tel.: (00 33) 5 46 99 16 88.
Vanessa Bell (pages 84 to 89): Charleston Farm House, Lewes, East Sussex BN8 6LL, England.
Tel.: (00 44) 1323 811 626
Website: www.charleston.org.uk
Rosenborg (pages 144 to 151): Rosenborg Castle, Oster Voldgade n°4A, 1350 Copenhagen, Denmark.
Tel.: (00 45) 33 15 32 86.

Translated from the French by David Radzinowicz Howell
Copy-editing: Christine Schultz-Touge
Color separation: Sele Offset
Typesetting: Claude-Olivier Four

Originally published as *Extravagances: l'art de vivre autrement*
© Flammarion, Paris, 2001
English-language edition © Flammarion, Paris, 2001

ISBN: 2-08010-642-2   FA0642-01-VII

Dépôt légal: October 2001

Printed in Italy